American Naval History, 1607–1865

American Naval History, 1607–1865

Overcoming the Colonial Legacy

JONATHAN R. DULL

University of Nebraska Press
Lincoln and London

© 2012 by the Board of Regents
of the University of Nebraska
All rights reserved. Manufactured
in the United States of America

♾

Library of Congress Cataloging-in-
Publication Data
Dull, Jonathan R., 1942–
American naval history, 1607–1865:
overcoming the colonial legacy/ Jonathan R. Dull.
p. cm. — (Studies in war, society, and
the military)
Includes bibliographical references
and index.
ISBN 978-0-8032-4052-0 (cloth: alk. paper) 1. United States—History, Naval—To 1900. I. Title.
E182.D89 2012
359.00973—dc23   2012026665

Set in Scala

Contents

Preface

Although there have been many splendid books on early American naval history, there is a need for a new survey of the subject, particularly one with a broad perspective. This book tries to meet that need. It begins before 1775 because at least until the time of the Civil War American naval history was influenced greatly by attitudes, practices, and conditions dating from American colonial history. It pays attention to other navies, particularly those of Britain and France, because American naval history is closely connected with British and French naval history. Although it can stand alone, it is intended as a companion volume to my book *The Age of the Ship of the Line: The British and French Navies, 1650–1865* (Lincoln: University of Nebraska Press, 2009). Both books are concerned with the ways navies reflect diplomatic, political, economic, and social developments.

Looking at American naval history from a wide perspective helps us to avoid reading the United States Navy's twentieth-century triumphs back into previous centuries. Until the Civil War, America was a minor naval power. During its first two major wars, the War of American Independence and the

War of 1812, the American navy was virtually annihilated. It is true that the navy fought a number of successful combats against individual enemy ships and even won battles on Lake Erie and Lake Champlain during the War of 1812. On balance, however, the record of the American navy during the age of sail was not very impressive, particularly in comparison with the British navy, which twice virtually swept it from the sea. Given America's enormous resources and growing population, its navy generally was undersized and poorly funded. Its participation in the Civil War of 1861–65 was very different. The navy suddenly expanded hugely and performed wonders against an extremely dangerous enemy. Although the navy then languished for a couple of decades, the foundations of American naval power had been established. Once America decided it wanted a modern navy, it was able to build one in fairly short order. In the twentieth century it became first a major naval power and then the world's dominant naval power.

Why did it take almost a century for the United States to build its first large navy? As I will argue, it was largely due to the continuation of traditions established in America's colonial past, such as localism and sectionalism, an obsession with the frontier and territorial expansion, and an aversion to strong central government and taxation. By weakening the power of the states, expanding American industry, and strengthening the federal government, the Lincoln administration finally made possible America's rise as a naval power.

In writing this book I have benefited from the work of numerous fine historians, including my friends John Hattendorf, Bill Fowler, Thomas Schaeper, Denver Brunsman, and Jim Bradford; its mistakes are my own. I also wish all too belatedly to acknowledge the encouragement given to me by a model naval officer, Lieutenant Commander Jay Arnold, executive officer of the USS *Duncan* (DDR 874), aboard which I served in 1964–66. As with previous books I wish to thank my wonderful family, particularly my wife, Susan Kruger, and children, Veronica Lamka, Robert Dull, Max Kruger-Dull, and Anna Kruger-Dull. I dedicate this book to two history buffs, my nephews Peter and John Hamburger.

American Naval History, 1607–1865

ONE

The American Colonies and the British Navy, 1607–1775

The naval great powers during the age of sailing ship warfare that ended in the middle of the nineteenth century were, with the exception of Great Britain, not those of the great age of battleship and aircraft carrier warfare during the first half of the twentieth century. The other great sailing navies, those of France, Spain, and the Netherlands, played a relatively minor role during the twentieth century. Instead the British navy was joined by three newly arrived naval great powers: Japan, Germany, and the United States. All three launched major building programs during the final decades of the nineteenth century and quickly became prominent once the United States defeated Spain in 1898 and Japan defeated Russia in 1904–1905. The groundwork for this ascendancy was laid earlier, however. In the middle of the nineteenth century the governments of Germany, Japan, and the United States greatly increased their power. Henceforth they were able to use their economic growth to become naval great powers. The equivalent of the German unification of 1871 and Japan's Meiji Restoration of 1867–68 was the American Civil War.

Although the two decades after the end of the Civil War were a period of naval retrenchment, the Civil War had laid the foundation for the United States to overcome the attitudes, practices, and conditions that had hindered the growth of its navy. These hindrances were part of the legacy of America's colonial past.

Between the founding of Jamestown in 1607 and the beginning of the American Revolution in 1775, Britain's American colonies developed important shipping and fishing industries but undertook little independent naval activity. This period of subservience to the mother country and to the needs of the British navy was very influential, however, in the subsequent development of the American navy. The Revolution did not eliminate America's colonial legacy. For the United States to become a naval power, it had to overcome a number of the things it inherited from its colonial past: a weak industrial base compared with naval great powers like Britain and France, a distrust of government and hence a reliance on private enterprise, sectionalism and a preference for state government rather than national government, an inability or reluctance to raise by taxation the money necessary for military and naval activity, and an obsession with internal expansion that necessitated a substantial investment on the frontier rather than on the sea. All of these obstacles were present almost from the beginning of English settlement in North America.

II

The English colonization of North America began in 1607 (after earlier failures); the first permanent French colony was established a year later. Both Virginia and New France began as private business investments approved by the respective crowns. This was a change from the sixteenth-century Spanish model in which the rulers of Castile and Aragon played (at least in theory) a direct role in exploration and colonization. Soon, however, the French colony was taken over by the royal government and administered from Europe. In contrast the more than a dozen English colonies established between 1607 and 1732 differed not only from the colonies of other nations but even from one another.[1] Some colonies like Connecticut had their own charters and administered their own affairs under very loose government supervision. Others like Pennsylvania were run by proprietors, who had veto power over the decisions reached by their colonial assemblies. Still others like Virginia became royal colonies with a governor appointed by the crown. Even royal governors, however, had to share power with their locally elected assemblies, which, like the English House of Commons (or, after the 1707 union with Scotland, the British House of Commons), used their control over the budget to gain a share of political power.[2]

Over the course of the seventeenth and eighteenth centuries, the struggle for power between assemblies and their governors or proprietors left many Americans distrustful of executive authority; even the inhabitants of Connecticut and Rhode Island, where governors were popularly elected, distrusted the kings of England, who might take their charters from them. Moreover, the British government exercised its own veto power over most colonial legislation, using it, for example, to control the issuing of currency by individual colonies. Until the middle of the eighteenth century, however, British control over the North American colonies was administered loosely, largely because Britain was preoccupied with European affairs.[3] These colonies also were considered less important than the rich sugar-producing colonies of the Caribbean, such as Jamaica. Thus most American politics was local, and American political life, like American society, was dominated by wealthy local elites who resented interference from England.

The North American colonies were diverse not only politically but also socially, economically, culturally, and religiously, although over the course of the eighteenth century these differences became less marked.[4] A planter in the South using slaves to raise tobacco or rice for European markets had, for example, different views on politics and economics than did a small farmer in New England producing for a local market. The colonies did trade among themselves (usually by sea because long distances and primitive roads made it difficult and expensive to move products by land), but generally Great Britain and the Caribbean were their most important markets and the chief sources of their imports. Moreover, except for a relatively efficient intercolonial postal system, the American colonies lacked common institutions. What they did share was a desire for expansion into new lands. All too often this led to competition rather than cooperation, such as the attempted intrusions by Virginia and Connecticut into parts of Pennsylvania. Even in military matters, cooperation between colonies often was halfhearted or ineffectual.

War was a recurrent part of life in British North America. Most wars were fought against the Native American nations whose hunting grounds or agricultural settlements were coveted by British Americans. In the early days of settlement, the colonies were not self-supporting and depended on supplies sent from England by sea. Soon, however, they achieved a measure of self-sufficiency. They were able to fight Indian wars using troops they raised themselves. Fortunately for them, Indian opposition in the seventeenth and early eighteenth centuries was uncoordinated. Unlike the powerful sixteenth-century Aztec Empire of Mexico or the Inca Empire of Peru, the Indians encountered by the British were divided into many small tribes or confederations of tribes. By the late seventeenth century few contained more than 10,000 people. The colonists were able to exploit rivalries between the various Indian nations as well to make use of their own greater population and advanced weaponry.

More challenging, however, were wars conducted against neighboring Dutch, Spanish, and French colonies. These sometimes involved the use of ships. Seldom were enemy warships encountered, but for logistical reasons colonial wars often involved moving troops by sea, usually on transports provided by colonies like Massachusetts. Until the so-called French and Indian War of 1754–60, most soldiers in British America served in either the militia or colonial regiments. Their frequent target was the French colony of Acadia, located across the Bay of Fundy from Massachusetts. It was captured on several occasions by New England raiders, but until the 1713 Treaty of Utrecht it was returned to France each time that hostilities ended.

The French colonies initially were less of an obstacle to the English colonies than was the Dutch colony of New Netherland along the Hudson River, which separated the New England colonies from English colonies to the south. In 1664, during the second of three wars fought between the Netherlands and Britain in the mid-seventeenth century, a small English squadron captured the city of New Amsterdam and renamed it New York. During the next war a Dutch squadron recaptured the city and colony.[5] Fortunately for the English, the colony was returned to England when the war ended in 1674.

The Glorious Revolution of 1688 made William of Orange, ruler of the Netherlands, and his wife, Mary, daughter of the deposed James II, joint rulers of England. William's archenemy, Louis XIV of France, immediately became the enemy of England and soon went to war on behalf of the exiled James. The Nine Years' War (1689–97) was fought chiefly in Europe, but the New England colonies also participated. In 1690 they even mounted an attack against Quebec, the capital of New France, but the attack failed.[6]

The War of the Spanish Succession began in 1702. Another attack on Quebec was made in 1711, but most of the troops and the supporting warships were sent from England. Because of the ineptitude of the British commander, several transports were wrecked while ascending the St. Lawrence, and the attack was abandoned. An attack on Port Royal, the capital of Acadia, was successful, however. At the end of the war, Acadia was retained by Britain, although its borders were not defined in the 1713 peace treaty.[7] This treaty also confirmed both the accession of Louis's grandson to the Spanish throne and the retention of Florida by Spain. (During the war, troops from South Carolina had made an unsuccessful attack on the Spanish fort at St. Augustine while their Indian allies attacked the Spanish fort at Pensacola.)[8]

Soon after the war ended, France and Britain became allies. Tension in North America did not disappear, although it was moderated by the powerful Iroquois confederation, which acted as a buffer between the British and French colonies.[9] The French, meanwhile, built the large fortified city of Louisbourg on Isle Royale (now Cape Breton Island) as a shelter and support for their fishing fleet used in the Newfoundland and St. Lawrence fisheries.[10]

Thus far the North American colonies had played only a minor role in the great wars of Europe. Except for the abortive 1711 attack on Quebec, no large fleets had come to North American waters. Nonetheless, Britain's North American colonies did make significant, although mostly indirect, contributions to British naval strength. The ways in which the colonies did and did not participate in naval warfare affected the American navy once the colonies asserted their independence.

III

Most contemporaries saw trade between the British colonies and Britain itself as the major colonial contribution to British naval strength. The mother country's Navigation Acts channeled much of the colonies' overseas trade to the British West Indies or to Great Britain, as well as restricting that trade to ships built and manned in Britain or its colonies. The purpose of the Navigation Acts was threefold. They enriched the British treasury, fostered the development of the British economy, and provided for the training of British sailors. (It was too expensive for Britain's navy to maintain a large peacetime fleet for training purposes, so most sailors in the navy received their training aboard merchant ships or fishing vessels; the same, of course, was true for the French and Spanish navies.) By 1775, perhaps a quarter of British shipping tonnage was devoted to trade with British North America and the British West Indies; moreover, nearly a third of British merchant ships had been built in America, where shipbuilding costs were less than in Britain.[11]

The American colonies made other important contributions

to the mother country. They supplied raw materials, such as indigo for dying fabric, and were an increasingly important market for British manufactures and services such as banking. American grain, meat, and fish were vital to feeding the British West Indies, which devoted almost all their acreage to crops for export such as sugar. Masts from New England and naval stores such as pitch, tar, and turpentine from the southern colonies were used by the British navy.[12] Colonial troops not only conducted military operations in North America but also assisted British troops in the Caribbean.

Although the British colonies in North America were important to the British economy in general and the navy in particular, there were certain areas in which they were not given the chance to contribute, were not capable of contributing, or did not choose to contribute. This would hinder naval development once America became independent.

First, the American colonies were given few opportunities to build warships for the British navy because their ships had a poor reputation for durability; the colonies, however, were allowed to repair British warships and to convert merchant ships into warships. Although the British navy contracted to build many warships in private dockyards in Great Britain, it purchased only a few frigates (medium-sized warships of 22 to 44 guns) from American shipyards and none of the larger ships of the line that were the chief component of naval power.[13] The French built a couple of 60-gun ships of the line at Quebec, as well as some smaller ships, but these were poorly constructed. The only shipbuilding facility in the Western Hemisphere comparable to the great dockyards of Europe was at Havana, where the Spaniards, with access to tropical hardwoods, built some of the finest warships in the world.[14] The specialty of the British colonies was the privateer, a privately built, owned, and manned but government-sanctioned armed vessel used chiefly to capture enemy merchant ships. These were built for speed rather than endurance, and served only during wartime. Hundreds of American privateers were used during the wars of 1739–48 and 1756–63 against France and Spain. Although privateers also were used during the American Revolution, American shipyards then also had to build sturdy, heavily armed warships to match those of the British.[15]

Second, the economy of the British colonies was underdeveloped by Western European standards, partly because the British preferred to see them as providers of raw material and customers for British products rather than as rivals. Thus in 1775 there were only three iron foundries in New England capable of casting cannon for warships.[16] Americans also were short of gunpowder, cannon balls, and other necessities of naval warfare. The colonies' greatest shortage, however, was specie, the gold or silver necessary to provide financial backing for currency. When the colonies revolted against Britain, their first response was simply to print money without backing, the same response the Confederacy would adopt in 1861. In both cases the result was inflation and the eventual destruction of the currency's purchasing power. The American Revolution was saved from disaster by financial aid from abroad, but the American revolutionary navy, virtually unable to pay its sailors or replace its ship losses, faded into insignificance.

Third, although many Americas served aboard merchant ships or fishing boats, few had served as sailors in the British navy, and almost none had served as officers or naval administrators; only three of the American navy's original twenty-six captains had any prior experience in the British navy.[17] The

British navy periodically attempted to force American merchant sailors to serve (an imposition called impressment), but the Americans, claiming to be exempt from such service, refused. They received support from public officials and from crowds that often resorted to intimidation or even violence. Usually the British gave up the effort.[18] Merchant sailors could learn fairly quickly how to adjust to life aboard privateers or warships, so this was not a long-term obstacle to the development of an American navy. It was far more difficult, however, to turn merchant ship or privateer officers into naval officers. This problem would also face the French navy during the French Revolution, but it at least had a few veteran captains and other officers who were willing to serve. The first American navy had no one who had commanded a squadron of ships, let alone a fleet.[19] George Washington had the help of former British army officers like Charles Lee and Horatio Gates and foreign volunteers like "Baron" von Steuben and the marquis de Lafayette; the navy had only Pierre Landais, an emotionally unstable former French junior officer. It would take considerable time to develop officers capable of commanding a group of ships in combat.

IV

Except for brief hostilities against Spain (and against pirates) in the 1720s, Britain was at peace from 1713 until 1739. North America was a backwater for the British navy, which did little more than assign station ships, none larger than a frigate, to Boston, New York, Charleston, Virginia, and eventually Savannah.[20] The colonies did not have permanent armies or navies, and there was not even a maritime equivalent to the rudimentary military training provided by colonial militias.

This period of peace ended when Britain declared war against Spain in 1739. The colonies participated enthusiastically, but the initial results were disastrous. Thousands of American provincial troops joined British troops in an attack on the fortified seaport of Cartagena de Indias on the northern coast of South America. The attack, supported by a very large British fleet, failed, and many of the Americans died of disease. Provincial troops from Georgia and South Carolina supported by British frigates also were unsuccessful in an attack on St. Augustine.[21] The Spaniards attempted to retaliate with an attack on Georgia in preparation for an attack on South Carolina, but the other British colonies were not threatened except by Spanish privateers. When France entered the war in 1744, New York and the New England colonies were menaced by attack from the Indian allies of New France. Massachusetts governor William Shirley organized an army of New England provincial troops to attack the great fortress of Louisbourg. Although he was able to assemble a troop convoy and arrange an escort of Massachusetts navy vessels, he needed the assistance of the British navy. He appealed for help to Commodore Peter Warren, who commanded a small squadron at Antigua in the British West Indies. Warren had spent many years in America, had an American wife, and had participated in the St. Augustine attack. He brought two small ships of the line and two frigates to Nova Scotia, where he rendezvoused with the New Englanders. The attack on Louisbourg caught the French by surprise, and the city was captured after a seven-week siege. British Americans had won their first great battle, albeit with the help of the British navy. To their disappointment Louisbourg was returned to France when peace was concluded in 1748, but the border between the British and French colonies remained tense.[22]

Neither the British nor the French government wished for another war, but the situation in North America was volatile. As in 1713, the peace negotiations had failed to define the limits of Acadia and had left the task of delineating the border between New France (including Canada and Acadia) and the British colonies to a bilateral border commission. The British and French governments failed to come to a general agreement on the issues between them, and the commission's discussions proved more divisive than helpful.[23] The recent war had disrupted French trade with Indian nations south of the Great Lakes. British American traders and land companies moved to fill the vacuum. A group of Virginia land speculators sought to open western Pennsylvania to settlement. This led to armed confrontations between Canadian troops and Virginia volunteers near what today is Pittsburgh. Subsequent negotiations between the British and French governments failed to resolve the dispute. In 1755 both governments sent troops to North America, and open hostilities soon began.[24]

The British colonies were unprepared for war. As recent events had demonstrated, they did not even respect one another's borders. Benjamin Franklin proposed that the colonies establish a joint military command, but his suggestion was rejected by both the British government and colonial assemblies.[25]

The new war was far wider in scope than previous colonial wars. The British and French sent regular infantry battalions and large fleets to North America. Their respective colonists played a subordinate role in the war, although large numbers of Canadian and American volunteers and militiamen served beside the regulars; during the decisive campaign of 1759, for example, almost 20,000 American troops served with a similar number of British soldiers, while some 10,000 Canadian militiamen were among the 15,000 troops opposing them.[26] Recruitment of American provincial troops was greatly aided by the British government's willingness to partly subsidize them, thereby neutralizing American suspicion, disunity, and reluctance to raise taxes. A major factor in the eventual British triumph was the overwhelming numerical superiority of the British navy. The colonists did provide troop transports for an unsuccessful attack on Louisbourg in 1757, but many transports for the successful campaigns of the following two years against Louisbourg and Quebec were sent to American ports from England. Most American sailors worked aboard merchant ships or privateers.

Other British attacks such as those against Fort Niagara and Montreal made use of waterways such as Lake Ontario, Lake George, Lake Champlain, and the St. Lawrence River.[27] The ships ranged from small boats to warships carrying as many as 18 cannon. This was an important precedent; significant naval actions on inland waters would occur during the wars of 1775–83, 1812–15, and 1861–65.

v

The war ended with the French being driven from the North American continent. The British victory, however, was even more destabilizing than had been the indecisive previous war. It was followed almost immediately by a major Indian war in 1763–64. Worse still, it disrupted relations between the British colonists and the government in Britain. For several decades the government in London had used the colonies as a source of patronage, while allowing colonial legislatures a considerable degree of autonomy. It had angered American colonists by, among other things, restricting their manufacturing certain items and restricting their issuing currency. This was counterbalanced, however, by the protection afforded them by the British navy, as well as by their pride in being British subjects. They protested when they felt rules were being violated, such as by impressment of sailors in American ports, but generally their yoke was light enough to be tolerated. Benjamin Franklin, for example, sent to England by the Pennsylvania Assembly to seek redress against Pennsylvania proprietor Thomas Penn, considered himself simultaneously a Briton, an American, and a Pennsylvanian. He even lobbied to make Pennsylvania a royal colony.[28]

The war, however, altered the relationship between Britain and its American colonies. With the French threat gone, Americans no longer needed Britain for protection from European enemies (and came to see the British army as less a protection from Indians than as a menace to themselves). The war, moreover, had caused the British to adopt new policies such as sending British troops to America and had added greatly to the British national debt. The British government now expected the colonies to help bear the heavy cost of policing the frontier. Furthermore, British authorities were outraged at the colonists for their massive illegal trade with the French West Indies during the war against France.[29] They now took action to curtail smuggling and to force compliance with the Navigation Acts, including the deployment of a large number of small warships in American waters.[30] Americans attempted to evade British trade restrictions and even retaliated against British warships, including burning the schooner *Gaspee* (one of fifteen such ships purchased in America by the British navy between 1764 and 1775).[31] They began to view Parliament as corrupt, more as a tyrannical European government than as a protector of their interests.

The decisive event in the breakdown of relations between Britain and its colonies was the so-called Boston Tea Party of December 1773. This destruction of tea sent to America by the British East India Company prompted Parliament to retaliate by passing the Coercive Acts, including the closing of Boston Harbor and numerous other American ports. Americans began preparing for armed resistance, smuggling gunpowder from Europe and the West Indies, and seizing cannon from minor British military posts.[32] Open hostilities began in April 1775 when a British army detachment from Boston attempted to seize gunpowder from the neighboring towns of Lexington and Concord. Americans now faced not only the British army in Boston but the entire British navy. They would also have to deal with the legacies of their own past: rivalries among the different states and regions of the country, distrust of central government, a preference for printing money rather than paying taxes, a shortage of leaders with experience in European-style military and naval warfare, a rudimentary bureaucracy, and an unevenly developed economy.

TWO

The War against Britain, 1775–1783

I

In 1774 the North American colonies sent delegates to a Continental Congress that unsuccessfully petitioned George III to
lift the Coercive Acts. It reconvened in 1775, soon after the Battles of Lexington and Concord, now facing not only the threat
of expanded British military action but also serious potential
opposition within the colonies. Many Americans did not want
a confrontation with the king or Parliament. Resistance, moreover, would require the thirteen colonies to cooperate with
each other, to cede some of their powers to Congress, and to
raise money for self-defense, all of which was controversial.
The most frightening aspect of the crisis was the danger that
Britain would not agree to a peaceful resolution of the dispute,
leaving the Americans to face the world's most powerful navy
and an experienced, powerful army. Not surprisingly, all but a
few radicals like Patrick Henry hoped for an accommodation
with the British government. Even Benjamin Franklin, newly returned to America after unsuccessful negotiations with
intermediaries in contact with the British government, was
willing to make a final effort to avert open warfare.[1]

In previous crises, such as the 1765–66 Stamp Act dispute, the colonies had obtained concessions from the British government by boycotting British goods. Congress again petitioned the king for relief, while hoping that the progressive implementation of non-importation, non-exportation, and non-consumption of goods from Britain would exert enough economic pressure to cause the British government to back down. The effort was hopeless. The king, Parliament and even most of the British public were eager to restore the mother country's authority over its colonies by whatever coercive methods were necessary. The king declared the colonies in rebellion, authorized seizure of their ships, and began assembling troops to reinforce those already in America. Most of them were in Boston; during the previous winter the British had even sent two of their four regiments in Canada to reinforce its garrison. The British navy could do little more than protect Boston Harbor and incoming ships; at the beginning of 1775, its North American squadron consisted of only three ships of the line, one 50-gun ship, one 28-gun frigate, and nineteen ships of 20 or fewer cannon, far too small a force to blockade the American coast.[2]

In the aftermath of Lexington and Concord, militiamen from New England began a blockade of Boston, a city on a peninsula connected to the mainland by a narrow causeway. General Thomas Gage, the British commander, sought to break the blockade by seizing Bunker Hill and Breed's Hill on the Charlestown Peninsula north of the city. The June 17 attack was successful, but cost the British 1,000 casualties. The stalemate resumed; the Americans lacked cannon while the British did not have enough troops to risk another attack. Meanwhile, Congress was anxious to demonstrate that the struggle was not New England's alone, so it elected George Washington to command the Continental army opposite Boston. He arrived at the army's headquarters in Cambridge, Massachusetts, in early July. Anxious to demonstrate that its cause was defensive, however, Congress delayed intercepting British shipping; Washington had to watch helplessly as the British received supplies from England and sent out a squadron that burned the port of Falmouth, some 100 miles northeast of Boston.[3]

Boston was not the only front, though. By withdrawing troops from Canada, the British had left exposed not only Canada itself but also the fortress of Ticonderoga on Lake Champlain. It was the major post along the Richelieu River to Lake Champlain to Lake George route by which troops could move between the St. Lawrence River and the Hudson River. Not only was it strategically important but it also had almost 100 cannon, which would be a priceless acquisition to the American army. What made it an even more tempting target was that its garrison had fewer than fifty men.

On May 10 the fort was captured without bloodshed by a force of some eighty "Green Mountain Boys" led by Ethan Allen and Massachusetts troops led by Benedict Arnold. A smaller detachment sent to the southern end of Lake Champlain captured the boatyard at Skenesborough and a trading schooner, both of which were owned by a British supporter. Arnold embarked troops aboard the schooner, sailed to the northern end of the lake, and captured a weakly garrisoned British fort and a sloop. With the two ships, renamed *Liberty* and *Enterprise* and armed, respectively, with 8 and 12 cannon, the Americans had complete control of the lake and could begin building small warships at Skenesborough. Most were gunboats, either 50- or 60-foot gondolas or 70- to 80-foot galleys, carrying both masts for sails and sweeps (oars) for rowing and armed with 3 to 10 cannon.[4] The first American navy thus was on fresh water rather than salt water, was manned by soldiers, and was commanded by Arnold, who had been commissioned a colonel by the Massachusetts Committee of Safety. Control of the lake permitted the transport of some 60 cannon removed from Ticonderoga part of the way to Cambridge. Transported the rest of the distance by sled, the cannon arrived at the beginning of March 1776.

Montreal was at the mercy of whoever controlled Lake Champlain. In 1759 the French had controlled the lake and forced the British to take the time to build a fleet, thereby saving Montreal from capture; the following year the British controlled the lake and captured the city. In 1775 Congress quickly abandoned its scruples about remaining on the defensive and approved an attack via the lake on Montreal; meanwhile Washington sent a second army up the Kennebec River to attack Quebec. (Escorted by ships of the Massachusetts navy, the troops were sent to the mouth of the Kennebec by sea.) After Montreal was captured without a fight, the two armies met at the walls of Quebec. They unsuccessfully stormed the city and were driven out of Canada the following year after a fruitless siege of Quebec. This attempt to seize Canada for the good of the Canadians had colonial as well as British antecedents and would be repeated in 1812; indeed, the expansionism that has played such an important role in American history is one of the most significant parts of its colonial legacy.[5]

Meanwhile Washington's patience gave out. At the end of the summer of 1775 he fitted out his own warship, the schooner *Hannah*, which was converted into a 4-gun warship to cruise against British shipping, using soldiers and officers from Washington's army. Although the *Hannah*'s career was brief and undistinguished, Washington decided to make a larger effort. He fitted out half a dozen schooners, using the ports of Beverly to the north of Boston and Plymouth to its south. He had not awaited congressional approval, but he received it retroactively. Pennsylvania, Connecticut, Rhode Island, and South Carolina formed their own navies (followed eventually by those of the other states), and privateers began cruising as well. At the beginning of November, Congress finally decided to purchase four merchant ships at Philadelphia for conversion into warships. These became the first warships of the Continental navy: the *Alfred*, 24 cannon, *Columbus*, 20, *Andrew Doria*, 14, and *Cabot*, 14. By the end of the year Congress had acquired four more ships: the *Providence*, 12, was purchased in Rhode Island, and the *Hornet*, 10, *Wasp*, 8, and *Fly*, 8, were purchased at Baltimore. It selected a naval committee to supervise the fleet and named a commodore, Esek Hopkins, a former slave ship captain and the brother of a naval committee member, to command it.

Congress ordered Hopkins to clear the British from Chesapeake Bay if possible. He sailed on 17 February 1776, but instead of the Chesapeake he went to the Bahamas, where he captured Nassau, seizing a substantial haul of munitions, including about 100 cannon. On the return voyage his ships encountered HMS *Glasgow*, 20, off Newport but failed to capture it.

If Hopkins's entire fleet could not capture one British warship, there was no hope of challenging the British fleet at Boston. By late 1775 it consisted of several ships of the line, half a dozen frigates, and nearly twenty smaller warships. Instead, Washington's schooners, the state navies, and privateers sought to capture the supply ships and transports on which the blockaded British garrison at Boston depended; meanwhile Pennsylvania began constructing a navy to defend the Delaware.[6] On 29 November 1775, Washington's schooner *Lee*, 6, took the most important prize of the entire war. It captured the munitions ship *Nancy*, en route to Boston with a cargo of all the equipment necessary for outfitting enough artillery for an army.[7] Without this cargo the artillery brought from Ticonderoga would have done little good. With it, all that Washington needed to do was await the cannon. Once it arrived, the British garrison of Boston was doomed.

II

Even before the departure of Hopkins's fleet, Congress decided to build its own warships. In doing so it established two of the most enduring traditions in American defense spending, those of selecting the most expensive weapon systems possible and of spreading the contracts among the various states in order to win political support. On 13 December 1775 it authorized the construction of five 32-gun frigates, five 28-gun frigates, and three 24-gun frigates. The following November it authorized the construction of three 74-gun ships of the line and five 36-gun frigates. Only one of the ships of the line, the *America*, was built, although before it was finished it was given to France to replace a French ship of the line shipwrecked off Boston. It was a convenient excuse to get rid of a ship that the Continental navy did not have the sailors to man; it would have required a crew of more than 600, double that of the largest American frigate. Unfortunately, the *America* was built of unseasoned wood; within a few years the French navy had to remove it from service.[8] Moreover, only three of the later frigates were built, although two others, the *Deane* (later renamed

Hague), 32, and *Queen of France*, 28, were purchased in France. For political reasons Congress chose to construct the frigates at a number of shipyards. Four of the sixteen frigates (the *Randolph*, 32, *Washington*, 32, *Effingham*, 28, and *Delaware*, 24) were built at Philadelphia, two (*Bourbon*, 28, and *Trumbull*, 28) at Chatham (now Portland), Connecticut, two (*Hancock*, 32, and *Boston*, 28) at Newburyport, Massachusetts, two (*Warren*, 32, and *Providence*, 28) at Providence, Rhode Island, two (*Congress*, 28, and *Montgomery*, 24) at Poughkeepsie, New York, and one each at Portsmouth, New Hampshire (*Raleigh*, 32), Fells Point, Maryland (*Virginia*, 28), Salisbury, Massachusetts (*Alliance*, 36), and Norwich, Connecticut (*Confederacy*, 36). The *America* also was built at Portsmouth.[9]

By European standards this was not a large building program; from 1775 through 1782 the British navy built thirty-nine ships of the line of 64–90 cannon, nine 50-gun ships, and sixty-two frigates, while the French navy built thirty-four ships of the line and forty-six frigates.[10] It was, however, overly ambitious for a country as yet underdeveloped. The frigates were surprisingly well designed, as American shipyards had experience repairing British frigates. The American ships resembled British ones, although they were somewhat larger. Like American merchant ships they were generally quite fast, but may not have been very durable. We cannot know for certain. A well-built frigate could last ten years, but none of the American ships served that long, including the time many of them spent in British service. The problem was the burden they put on American financial, material, and human resources. They demanded money, cannon, and sailors—all of which were in short supply. Moreover they generally did not give equivalent value for their cost. Six of them never reached the ocean:

the *Congress* and *Montgomery*, destroyed to prevent their capture,[11] the *Delaware, Effingham*, and *Washington*, either captured or burned by the British in the Delaware River,[12] and the
Bourbon, not launched until the war was over and then sold
while still incomplete. Ten were captured or destroyed during the war (the *Raleigh, Randolph*, and *Hancock* in 1777, the
Virginia in 1778, the *Warren* in 1779, the *Boston, Providence*,
and *Queen of France* in 1780, and the *Confederacy* and *Trumbull* in 1781). Only the *Hague* and *Alliance* survived the war;
the former was sold in 1783 and the latter in 1785. In return
they captured only one British frigate, the *Fox*, which was recaptured after eleven days, and fewer than 100 small British
warships, privateers, and merchant ships. Smaller Continental navy warships also took fewer than 100 prizes.[13]

The American-built frigates were built for pursuit of prizes and escape from warships rather than for combat. No more
than three ever served together. The only major operations in
which they served were disastrous. An unsuccessful 1779 attack on a British post in the Penobscot River cost not only the
Warren but also a Continental navy sloop of war, three Massachusetts navy warships, and more than thirty privateers and
transports.[14] The following year the *Boston, Providence, Queen
of France*, and the sloop of war *Ranger*, 18, were lost in the unsuccessful defense of Charleston, South Carolina.[15]

The two largest American warships were not part of the
Continental navy. The *Bonhomme Richard*, 40, was converted from a French merchant ship used in the East India trade.
It was the flagship of a squadron of seven ships financed by
Louis XVI. The squadron contained a warship of the Continental navy (the frigate *Alliance*), a warship of the French navy
(the cutter *Cerf*, 18), three warships owned by the king but not

part of the French navy (the *Bonhomme Richard*, the frigate *Pallas*, 32, and corvette *Vengeance*, 12), and two privateers that separated from the squadron soon after sailing. There was a long history of squadrons privately financed by the kings of France in order to make money and to assist the French navy; one such squadron captured the great port of Cartagena de Indias in 1697.[16] In this case there were also more generous motives involved, those of providing assistance to the United States and of furnishing a ship for the celebrated American captain John Paul Jones to command. The squadron also was intended to act as a diversion in order to assist a Franco-Spanish fleet in the English Channel, although it sailed too late to be of help. The squadron sailed around Ireland and Scotland into the North Sea, capturing more than a dozen prizes. On 20 September 1779, off the east coast of England, it encountered a large convoy of ships from the Baltic escorted by only two warships. The British warships interposed themselves between their convoy and Jones's squadron, enabling the valuable merchant ships to escape. The sloop of war *Countess of Scarborough*, 20, subsequently was captured by the *Pallas*, while the frigate *Serapis*, 44, was captured by the *Bonhomme Richard*. During the battle the *Alliance* tried to aid the *Bonhomme Richard*, but some of her shot hit Jones's ship, which was locked to the *Serapis*; Jones later falsely accused Pierre Landais, the French-born captain of the *Alliance*, of trying to aid the *Serapis*. The squadron and its prizes sailed to a Dutch port, but the badly damaged *Bonhomme Richard* had to be abandoned. The battle was a boost to American morale, but accomplished little else for the cause. The prisoners were turned over to the French, and the *Serapis* was acquired at auction by Louis XVI. Jones was a superb ship handler and highly skilled at single ship combat, but too inexperienced and arrogant to be an effective squadron commander.[17]

The Dutch-built frigate *Indien*, 40, also became very celebrated, particularly for its huge size, which may have had an influence on subsequent American ship design. It was leased to the South Carolina navy and renamed the *South Carolina*. Although it failed in its initial mission of escorting supply ships from Amsterdam to America, it did escort a Spanish expeditionary force that captured Nassau in the Bahamas in 1782. (When peace was signed, the Spaniards exchanged the Bahamas for the eastern portion of Florida.) The *South Carolina* went to Philadelphia and later was captured by a British squadron.[18]

The Continental navy did have some accomplishments in addition to the ships it captured. The brig *Reprisal* took Benjamin Franklin to France, the frigate *Boston* took John Adams to France, and the frigate *Confederacy* took John Jay to Martinique, where he was able to find passage on a French frigate to Spain. The *Alliance* carried Colonel John Laurens on a vital diplomatic mission to France, as well as bringing Spanish silver coins to America. The heroism of captains like John Paul Jones fostered patriotism, and the act of creating a navy helped American unity. Nonetheless the building program was overly expensive given the more vital needs of the Continental army and the shaky condition of American finances. Something more than the gunboats of Lake Champlain was needed, but the ship of the line and eighteen frigates launched or purchased put too much of a strain on the Continental Congress's finances. Perhaps most useful would have been a force with fewer frigates and more brigs and sloops of war like the *Reprisal* and *Ranger*.[19] Whatever the case, the Continental navy faced insuperable odds. In spite of the courage of its officers and sailors, the skill of its shipbuilders, and the dedication of those who attempted to administer its affairs, the navy had no way of overcoming the superior administration, technology, training, and experience of the British navy. Above all it was hopelessly outnumbered.

III

The naval history of the War of Independence is not only the history of the Continental navy. The Continental army, the state navies, and American privateers played important roles, too. The most vital contribution to American independence, however, was made by the French navy and its allies, the navies of Spain and the Netherlands.

The most useful American sailors were not those who served in the Continental navy but those who served in the Continental army. By good fortune Washington's army contained a regiment of seafarers from Marblehead, Massachusetts, commanded by a local ship owner and merchant, Colonel John Glover. Glover was a leader in the formation of Washington's schooner squadron, which was manned by officers and soldiers from his regiment. Even more vital were the services of Glover's regiments during the campaign of 1776. It was Glover's men (and a second regiment also composed of former sailors) who rescued Washington's army after its defeat on Long Island, rowing the soldiers across New York Harbor. They also helped row Washington's army across the Delaware before its victory at Trenton.[20]

The same year the squadron on Lake Champlain commanded by General Benedict Arnold and manned by soldiers of the Continental army disrupted a British attack from Canada. It forced British General Guy Carleton to portage an entire squadron around the rapids of the Richelieu River, which connects Lake Champlain to the St. Lawrence River. It took until October for Carleton to reassemble his squadron and then sail in pursuit of Arnold. The resulting Battle of Valcour Island was a British victory, but it came too late in the year for Carleton to attack Fort Ticonderoga. Instead, the fort was spared until the following year when the Americans were better prepared to resist an invasion from Canada.[21]

While the Americans fought Burgoyne's 1777 invasion, the Pennsylvania navy was fighting another British offensive. Its tiny gunboats, similar to those on Lake Champlain, destroyed a grounded British ship of the line, the *Augusta*, 64. It also forced the British to spend seven weeks after General William Howe's capture of Philadelphia reducing the American forts south of the city on either side of the Delaware. Not until 16 November 1777 was the Delaware open to shipping, too late for the British army to continue its campaign against the American army west of Philadelphia.[22]

The some 2,000 privateers commissioned by Congress or the states also played an important part in the war, capturing more than 2,200 British merchant ships (not including those recaptured by the British).[23] This forced the British to divert ships for convoy protection, added to insurance rates, and possibly contributed to the war weariness that finally undermined Lord North's government in 1782. Privateering gave some Americans a financial incentive to support the war and helped keep the economy from collapsing. On the other hand, it made it very difficult to man the ships of the Continental navy and state navies. It cost the lives of thousands of captured American sailors, who were crammed aboard British prison ships and left to die. It increased the gulf between rich and poor and fostered greed and selfishness. The record is so mixed that it is difficult to strike a balance.[24] It seems, however, that its effect on the British war effort was insignificant in comparison with the British struggle against the navies of France, Spain, and the Netherlands.

The Continental Congress naively had hoped that the prospect of American trade would be enough to bring help from Europe. Instead it had to sign a treaty of alliance with France in conjunction with a commercial treaty. France entered the war in 1778, followed in 1779 by Spain and in 1780 by the Netherlands; together their three navies outnumbered the British. I discuss the war between the British navy and its European enemies in the companion book to this, *The Age of the Ship of the Line: The British and French Navies, 1650–1815*. Suffice it to say here that after several indecisive campaigns, the United States was saved from total economic collapse in 1781 by the victory at Yorktown, which was made possible by the triumph of the French navy over the British off the entrance to Chesapeake Bay.[25] That victory in turn was largely the product of the pressure applied in European waters by the fleets of Spain and the Netherlands as well as France. The following year peace commissioners Benjamin Franklin, John Adams, and John Jay were able to arrange highly favorable terms by agreeing in all but name to a separate treaty with Britain. France, Spain, and the Netherlands subsequently received less favorable terms. Spain recovered Florida and Minorca, but France achieved little more than seeing Britain temporarily weakened by the loss of its monopoly of American trade. Very soon, however, Britain, able to undersell France, recovered a dominant share of American trade.

The United States had achieved its independence and received favorable boundaries. This outcome largely was determined by sea power, but it was mostly the power of European navies, even though significant contributions to American independence were made by Washington's schooners, the gunboats of Lake Champlain and the Delaware, and the sailor-soldiers of Glover's regiment.

The difficulties that the Continental Congress and its navy encountered were largely an outgrowth of America's colonial legacy. In particular the War of Independence resembled the previous war of 1755–60. In both wars, rivers and lakes were important theaters of war, and on these inland bodies of water it was the army that did the fighting. In both wars, too, Americans were dependent on European navies, the British navy in the earlier war, the French navy and its allies in the latter. In both wars most American sailors served on privateers or on ships of colonial or state navies. The importance of privateers reflected the American preference for private enterprise and distrust of central governments; moreover, as an able historian of the period comments, the enthusiasm at the beginning of the Revolution soon waned and, as soon as they could, Americans reverted to their usual pattern of putting private interests above the collective public interest.[26]

The weakness of the Continental navy largely was a question of money. Congress lacked its own source of funds and was dependent on the states. The states were slow to pay, in part because of the reluctance of their citizens to pay taxes; eventually Congress had to turn to France and the Netherlands for financial assistance. The Continental navy was unable to match the pay offered by privateers, let alone the relative freedom enjoyed by privateer sailors. Moreover, the Continental navy suffered from America's prior dependence on the British navy. Few of its captains had served in the British navy, and none had experience directing a squadron, let alone a fleet.

Finally, the Continental navy lacked the bureaucracy, shore establishment, and infrastructure of a European navy. For example, America had no major dockyard; there was not a single dry dock in the United States. There also were no Americans experienced in naval administration; the system of committees and boards established by the Continental Congress to run the navy finally broke down, and the navy was taken over as a collateral responsibility by Robert Morris, the American superintendent of finance.[27] Navy captains and sailors were brave and in some cases quite capable, but the navy in general resembled a European navy of the mid-seventeenth century. In the future the American navy would be thrown on its own resources. The United States would have to create a navy more effective and modern than the Continental navy had been.

THREE

A New Navy Fights France and the Barbary States, 1783–1805

I

American independence, achieved with great difficulty, was incomplete and tentative. International law provided little protection in the eighteenth-century Atlantic world. Weak states survived chiefly because of the mutual jealousy of their stronger neighbors. This was no guarantee; between 1772 and 1795 Poland was partitioned three times and finally disappeared. The end of the War of Independence provided the United States with a breathing spell because the great naval powers— Britain, France, and Spain—were exhausted financially. The United States could not count, however, on the respite lasting more than a few years. Its best defenses were geographical: its distance from Europe, its huge size, and the fact that its population centers were small and scattered. In spite of these advantages it had come close to being starved into submission during the war. Only French money, troops, and warships had prevented its economic collapse.[1]

The United States was reminded quickly of its weakness. After the signing of a provisional general peace on 20 January 1783, commissioners Benjamin Franklin, John Adams, and John Jay expected to negotiate a treaty that would ensure America's economic independence. The British not only refused to make any changes to the preliminary peace agreement but, in July 1783, closed the British West Indies to American shipping.[2] American shipbuilding and commerce underwent steep declines. The Americans had no commercial weapons with which to retaliate. Starved of luxury items, consumers rushed to purchase British goods as soon as the first British ships reached American ports in early 1783. Individual states blocked any attempt at common action against Britain, hoping instead to take advantage of their neighboring states' distress. Congress could impose neither taxes nor a common commercial policy without the unanimous consent of the states, which proved impossible to obtain. Indeed, Congress was virtually as impotent as the Diet of Poland, another political body whose need for unanimous consent led to Poland's domination by its neighbors and eventual extinction. With no navy, virtually no revenue, and an army of only about 1,000 soldiers borrowed from the states, Congress was unable to pay its debts or defend American territory.[3]

Not surprisingly the United States was treated with contempt by foreign powers. The Spanish government refused to allow American shipping access to New Orleans, cutting off trade via the Mississippi River. The British government refused to evacuate nine frontier posts within the United States until Americans paid their debts to British merchants.[4] The last warship of the Continental navy, the frigate *Alliance*, was sold in 1785, leaving no protection for merchant ships. American ships trading with Europe were vulnerable to corsairs from the Barbary States (the regencies of Morocco, Algiers, Tripoli, and Tunis). Nominally tributaries of the Ottoman Empire, they were largely independent of control from Constantinople. They supported themselves by exacting tribute from the states of Europe or by seizing the ships of those states that didn't pay tribute and then enslaving their crews.[5] Before the war American ships had been protected by the British navy; now they were no longer safe. In October 1784 the merchant ship *Betsey* was captured by a corsair from Morocco. In July 1785 corsairs from Algiers took the *Maria* and *Dolphin* and imprisoned their crews. Fortunately the ruler of Morocco, Sultan Muhammad ibn Abdallah, wishing his country to develop into a trading state, was willing to negotiate. In July 1786 he signed a commercial agreement with the United States and released his hostages; negotiations with Algiers failed, however, and the American captives remained enslaved.[6]

The navy of Portugal, which was at war with Algiers, kept Algerian corsairs from passing through the Straits of Gibraltar, but American trade with the Mediterranean virtually disappeared.

These various humiliations greatly wounded American pride. The United States, a victim of what we now call neocolonialism, had become a virtual economic satellite of Great Britain. The final blow to the Continental Congress came in 1786 when Shays's Rebellion, a debtors' movement, challenged the authority of courts in Massachusetts and seemed to threaten the entire social order of the state. The following year a Constitutional Convention, meeting in Philadelphia, approved a constitution established to protect the United States from challengers of the social order and from foreign domination. The Continental Congress was replaced by a bicameral legislature, an independent executive, and a separate federal judiciary. Among other powers given to the new government was the authority to establish a navy.

This authority was not exercised immediately. Once the Constitution was accepted by the states and George Washington was elected as president, the government turned to its most pressing problems. It placed a tariff on foreign imports, providing steady revenue to the federal government and protecting American manufacturers from foreign competition. It also sent military expeditions to counter the most immediate military threat, a coalition of Indian nations north of the Ohio River. As yet, however, no steps were taken to help the hostages in Algiers or to establish a navy. America's only naval force was ten revenue cutters built for the Treasury Department's Revenue Marine between 1791 and 1793 to prevent smuggling and assist in the collection of import duties; like the ships of the U.S. Coast Guard, which succeeded it, they would serve beside the navy in time of war.[7]

George Washington's first term, largely free from foreign threats and extreme political divisions, solidified the new form of government. His second term, beginning in the spring of 1793, was more contentious. On 1 February 1793 the new revolutionary government of France, already at war with Prussia and Austria, declared war on Great Britain and the Netherlands; the following month it declared war on Spain. This was a great opportunity for neutral shipping, particularly that of the United States. During this period the tonnage of American shipping engaged in foreign trade tripled, while American imports and exports quadrupled.[8] Washington sought to take advantage of this opportunity by proclaiming neutrality and thereby keeping America out of the war and free to trade with both sides. Britain and France, as well as their respective American sympathizers, however, made it difficult to maintain this policy. Both attempted to interfere with American trade. The crisis that finally led to the establishment of a navy, however, was caused by a foreign power with whom no one sympathized: the regency of Algiers (although many Americans blamed Britain for precipitating the crisis).

II

On 1 April 1783 Jean-Antoine Salva, who worked at the French consulate in Algiers, wrote to warn Benjamin Franklin of the danger from corsairs. He enclosed a list of the current naval forces of Algiers: a 42-gun warship currently out of service, nine warships of 18–34 cannon, and ten ships powered by oars and mounting 2–4 cannon.[9] As long as the Portuguese navy patrolled the Straits of Gibraltar, the threat could be avoided by not sending merchant ships into the Mediterranean. In late 1793, however, Portugal signed a truce with Algiers arranged by the British consul in Algiers and removed its patrols. Algerian corsairs entered the Atlantic and quickly seized eleven American merchant ships.

Congress responded by passing the Naval Act of 1794, authorizing the construction of six frigates large enough to overwhelm any Algerian warship, the largest of which then carried 44 guns. Four of these frigates were to carry 44 cannon, while the other two were to carry 36 cannon. This was later amended; three of the frigates, the *Constitution, President*, and *United States*, were rated as carrying 44 cannon (although they carried more), and the other three, the *Constellation, Congress*, and *Chesapeake*, were rated as 36's.[10] As with the Continental navy, the contracts were spread around in order to win political support; the ships were to be built in Boston, New York, Philadelphia, Portsmouth (New Hampshire), Baltimore, and Norfolk, but this time by government employees in dockyards leased by the government. These frigates were designed by American architects including Joshua Humphrey, who also had been involved in the Revolutionary War construction program. Although they resembled British frigates, they, like their Revolutionary War predecessors, were adapted to American ideas, particularly the American obsessions with speed and with overcoming adversaries in single-ship combat.[11] The most famous were the 44's. They were similar in size to a 60-gun ship of the line of the previous generation, such as the *Panther*, launched in 1758 and not dismantled until 1787. They carried a crew slightly larger than the *Panther*'s 420, and like the *Panther*, their main battery mounted cannon firing a 24-pound cannonball.[12]

Although these were fine ships, their reputation is somewhat inflated. First, they were considerably larger than frigates carrying 12- or 18-pound cannon, but they were not the only frigates carrying 24-pounders. In 1797 the British launched two 44-gun frigates of this type (modeled after a captured French 44), and the French launched eight, mounting various numbers of cannon, in 1794 and 1795. The use of frigates mounting 44 smaller cannon was more long-standing; the *Serapis*, captured by the *Bonhomme Richard*, was a 44-gun frigate carrying 18-pounders.[13] Second, their great size was not an unmixed blessing. Because they were very long in relationship to their width, they were prone to structural weakening, a failing also of French ships of the line.[14] Finally they took a very long time to build, partly because of their size, but partly because they were built of material intended to be the best, including copper plates for their hulls imported from England and special building pieces made from live oak cut in the remote sea islands of Georgia.

The building of these ships took so long that none of them was complete when news arrived in March 1796 that peace had been signed with Algiers. The Naval Act of 1794 had specified that construction was to be stopped if a peace treaty were signed, but Congress relented. It agreed to complete (but not to provide crews for) the three ships whose construction was furthest advanced, the *United States, Constitution,* and *Constellation.* Construction of the others was suspended.[15] The treaty with Algiers obligated the United States not only to pay tribute but also to build a frigate and three small ships for the dey of Algiers. The frigate, the *Crescent,* was launched in June 1797, six weeks after the launching of the *United States,* but before the launching of the other two American frigates.[16] All three American frigates soon were needed. By the end of 1797 the United States faced the prospect of another unanticipated war.

III

Several years earlier, the United States had seemed on the verge of war with Great Britain. During the summer of 1793, a few months after the outbreak of the war between Britain and France, both of these powers authorized the capture of neutral ships carrying provisions to the ports of their enemy.[17] Edmond-Charles Genet, the maladroit French minister in Philadelphia, made many enemies for France by his personal attacks on President Washington and by his attempts to mount military operations against Britain from the United States. Genet also hoped to use three French ships of the line that were outfitting at New York after bringing a convoy from the French colony of St. Domingue, but instead they returned to France.[18] Nevertheless it was the British who most angered Americans. Over the winter of 1793–94, the British navy began seizing American merchant ships trading with the French West Indies, the British governor of Lower Canada encouraged representatives of the Miami Indian nation to resist the Americans, and the British consul at Algiers arranged the truce between Algiers and Portugal.[19] The impetus for the construction of the new navy thus was not only Algerian aggression against American shipping but also Britain's supposed duplicity.

During the early months of 1794, the French government repudiated Genet and changed its objectives. Facing potential starvation, it turned to the United States for food. French purchasing agents acquired 24 million pounds of flour that was loaded on some 130 to 140 French merchant ships in U.S. ports. In April these ships rendezvoused off the New Jersey coast with a French squadron containing two ships of the line and several smaller vessels. It managed to elude a British fleet off the French coast and to reach the port of Brest, although a French fleet sent to meet it was badly mauled by a British fleet on 1 June 1794. American ships also sailed to France, although a second French convoy was intercepted by the British off the U.S. coast in June.[20] When James Monroe arrived in Paris as the new minister (replacing Gouverneur Morris, who was far less sympathetic to the French Revolution), he was warmly welcomed. Almost simultaneously, however, John Jay, who was strongly pro-British and hostile to the French Revolution, arrived in London in hopes of preventing war between the United States and Great Britain.

On 19 November 1794 Jay signed a treaty with the British that conceded the two points they most desired: it permitted them to confiscate enemy property found aboard American ships, and it prohibited the sale in American ports of prizes made by French ships. In effect it ended the Franco-American treaties of 1778 and turned the United States into a British ally; for example, the British were able to purchase horses and provisions in the United States for their campaigns in the West Indies.[21] The Americans, in return, were granted a right of trade with the British West Indies so limited that Congress scornfully rejected that article of the treaty. However, the treaty was far less one-sided than it appeared. The British were generally willing to bend the application of their trade restrictions as long as the principle was respected, paying for the provisions they confiscated and returning ships improperly seized. They also made important concessions, such as finally turning over their posts in American territory and opening to American shipping their valuable trade with India. Equally important was what they did not commit to writing. Governors of the individual islands in the British West Indies repeatedly permitted trade with American ships. The British navy eventually reduced its seizure (impressment) of sailors taken from American merchant ships on suspicion of their having been born in Great Britain, and British courts often freed captured American ships upon appeal.[22]

Monroe had reassured the French government of American support for its revolution. Even after learning of Jay's signing of a treaty, the French continued to believe in the goodwill of the American people, particularly Americans belonging to the emerging Republican Party of Jefferson and Madison. They believed, however, that Washington, Hamilton, and the rival Federalist Party were tools of the British. They watched with shock as Washington approved the Jay Treaty, the Senate ratified it, and the House of Representatives appropriated the money to implement it by the narrowest of margins. In July

1796 the French government informed Monroe that it considered its treaties with the United States broken and recalled its minister to Philadelphia without leave; a few months later it announced reprisals against American shipping. Its attempts to pressure the United States backfired when Jefferson was narrowly defeated by the Federalist presidential candidate, John Adams. During the winter following the 1796 election, French privateers from Guadeloupe and St. Domingue captured several hundred American ships, creating a crisis for the incoming president.[23]

President Adams responded to the crisis much as Washington had responded to the crisis caused by the British seizure of American ships three years previously. By now Monroe had been recalled, although the French refused to receive his replacement, the Federalist Charles C. Pinckney. Adams now named Pinckney, the Federalist John Marshall, and Adams's friend Elbridge Gerry, a moderate, to negotiate with France.

The mission was a failure. The Directory, the five-member French executive, had appointed the shrewd Charles-Maurice de Talleyrand-Périgord as foreign minister but had retained its control over foreign relations. It was content to continue seizing American ships, and Talleyrand himself was anxious to rid Gerry of his colleagues. At least in that he was successful. When his colleagues left Paris after negotiations failed, Gerry remained behind. Talleyrand created the impression, however, that the reason for the negotiations' failure was the American commissioners' refusal to pay him a bribe via his agents.[24]

When Adams released the details of the failed negotiations (referring to Talleyrand's agents as X, Y, and Z), Americans were outraged. In response to the French threat to American shipping, the frigates *United States*, *Constellation*, and *Constitution*

were launched in 1797. In the spring of 1798 Congress directed them to undertake active operations, authorized the purchase or construction of additional frigates and smaller warships, established the Department of the Navy, and finally
instructed the navy to capture any French warships preying
on shipping off the American coast.[25] There were not enough
votes in Congress to declare war on France, and the use of privateers was not authorized, but a "quasi" or partial war began
that summer.

IV

The establishment of the Navy Department with a secretary
holding cabinet rank was a large step toward a modern, permanent navy. Fortunately the first secretary of the navy, the
Maryland merchant Benjamin Stoddert, was astute, well organized, creative, and indefatigable.[26] Within three years he
added more ships to the navy than had been built or purchased during the eight years of the American Revolution. As
during the Revolution, the first new warships were converted
from merchant ships (either brigs or schooners): *Ganges*, 24,
George Washington, 24, *Baltimore*, 20, *Montezuma*, 20, *Delaware*, 20, *Herald*, 18, *Norfolk*, 18, *Richmond*, 18, and *Augusta*,
14. The largest of these often were called frigates because of
the number of guns they carried but should probably be count-
ed as sloops of war because of their weak construction. Eight
revenue cutters were also taken into naval service, while two
sloops of war (the *Maryland*, 20, and *Patapsco*, 20) and two
schooners (*Enterprise*, 12, and *Experiment*, 12) were constructed later. Congress approved building six ships of the line, but
only one was begun and none finished. The largest ships in
the navy were the fifteen frigates added to the three already

43

in service, many of them built with war bonds subscribed in port cities for their construction. In addition to the *President*, 44, *Congress*, 36, and *Chesapeake*, 36, already under construction, these were the *Philadelphia*, 36, *New York*, 36, *Essex*, 32, *Boston*, 28, *General Greene*, 28, *Adams*, 28, *John Adams*, 28, *Portsmouth*, 24, *Merrimack*, 24, *Connecticut*, 24, *Trumbull*, 24, and *Warren*, 24. As no more frigates were launched until 1814, these formed the heart of the navy not only during the present hostilities but also during the subsequent wars against Tripoli and Great Britain.

During the summer of 1798 the new navy quickly chased French privateers from the American coast. Stoddert realized that the best way to protect trade was to attack the enemy privateers in their West Indian bases. Over the next three years virtually every warship in the navy made at least one Caribbean cruise. (The major exception was the *Essex*, which escorted a convoy to the Indian Ocean and then brought a return convoy home.) The small ships were the most useful because they could operate in shallow waters, but the frigates were needed for protection from frigates of the regular French navy. Although at least seven French frigates (*Vengeance*, 48, *Africaine*, 44, *Sirène*, 42, *Pensée*, 42, *Volontaire*, 40, *Insurgente*, 40, and *Vestale*, 32) visited the Caribbean during the hostilities, they were poorly manned and not anxious for combat.[27] Captain Thomas Truxtun's *Constellation* captured the *Insurgente* (and later fought and nearly captured the *Vengeance*), but there were unexpected consequences. French naval minister Eustache Bruix supported Talleyrand's attempts to prevent open war and had attempted to restrict the Caribbean privateers; news of the capture of the *Insurgente* caused him to reverse his policy.[28]

Aided by the British navy, the American navy gradually reduced the toll of merchant ship captures. It also provided a squadron to assist François-Dominique Toussaint Louverture, the ex-slave who had led the Caribbean colony of St. Domingue to virtual independence from France; the *General Greene* even bombarded the forces of one of Toussaint Louverture's rivals.[29] Meanwhile Adams and Talleyrand were working to end the hostilities. The 1799 coup that made Napoleon Bonaparte the first consul and effective ruler of France helped; Napoleon wanted to bring the war to an end so that he could recapture St. Domingue. A new set of American commissioners finally reached France in 1800, and on 3 October the Convention of Mortfontaine brought the hostilities to an end. In effect the Americans abandoned claims to reimbursement for the losses to American shipping while the French agreed to end the Franco-American alliance and treaty of commerce of 1778. The new treaty also agreed to the principle of "free ships, free goods," meaning that enemy goods except for contraband could not be seized from neutral ships.

During his tenure Stoddert took a number of steps to professionalize the navy, including the purchase of navy yards at Boston, Brooklyn, Philadelphia, Washington, Portsmouth (New Hampshire), and Gosport (near Norfolk, Virginia). The election of 1800, however, brought into office Jefferson's Democratic Republicans, who were suspicious of navies and were obsessed with cutting government spending. One of President Adams's final acts was to reduce the size of the navy, lest Jefferson abolish it altogether. All but thirteen frigates (the *Constitution, President, United States, Congress, Constellation, Chesapeake, Philadelphia, New York, Essex, Boston, General Greene, Adams,* and *John Adams*) and one schooner (the *Enterprise*) were ordered to be sold. Only six frigates were kept on active duty, while most of the navy's officers were discharged from service. Moreover, a building program approved in 1799 that included six 74-gun ships of the line and two dry docks was abandoned. Unfortunately the greatly reduced peacetime navy almost immediately returned to war, this time against Tripoli, one of the Barbary States.

v

Following the 1795 treaty with Algiers, the United States had signed treaties with Tripoli in 1796 and Tunis in 1797. The money paid to them was substantially less than that paid to Algiers, however, and their rulers became discontented. On 14 May 1801 the pasha of Tripoli declared war on the United States.[30] President Jefferson did not learn of this for many months, but the warnings from the Mediterranean were sufficiently disturbing that soon after taking office he began preparing a "squadron of observation" for the Mediterranean. Its purpose was to prevent war or, if too late, to blockade any Barbary port whose ships had attacked American shipping. Jefferson had long advocated using force rather than paying tribute, but he was also concerned with economy, and half of the few remaining ships of the navy had been put in reserve. The squadron he sent (the *President*, 44, *Philadelphia*, 36, *Essex*, 32, and *Enterprise*, 12) was far too small to blockade a fortified harbor like Tripoli with its nearly 200 cannon and its numerous gunboats for harbor defense.[31] Furthermore the coast was poorly charted and extremely dangerous. On 31 October 1803 the *Philadelphia* ran aground off the harbor. Its crew was captured and held for ransom. Moreover, the Americans had no bases of their own and needed to refit and replenish in foreign ports like the great British base at Malta.

The war proved far more expensive than paying tribute. It took four years, requiring new squadrons to be sent every year. All of the navy's thirteen frigates except for the *General Greene* served at one time or another. The Americans even financed an army (with which a handful of American Marines served) that marched from Egypt halfway to the port of Tripoli with the idea of deposing the pasha in favor of his brother. On 3 June 1805 the pasha agreed to a treaty by which ransom was paid for the crew of the *Philadelphia*, but claims for future tribute were waived.[32]

The navy performed valiantly, but its record was mixed. Its attempts to bombard the city into surrender were unsuccessful. With the exception of Edward Preble (who commanded the squadron in 1803–1804), its commodores were undistinguished. Its individual ship captains and crews were excellent, however. The most celebrated ship captain was Stephen Decatur, who on the night of 16 February 1804 sailed a disguised ship into the harbor and boarded the *Philadelphia*, killing or driving away its small prize crew. Decatur and his men then burned the *Philadelphia*, reboarded their own ship, and escaped.[33] Because of their exploits Decatur and Preble became national heroes, and the war was treated as a great success. It revealed, however, the same weaknesses as in earlier wars. Lacking the infrastructure for a navy, Americans were dependent on the help of allies, in this case, the British at Gibraltar and Malta. Individual captains and crews sometimes were highly skilled, but the navy was inexperienced in fleet operations. Above all, it was very small. Tripoli had only one warship carrying more than 20 cannon and was by far the weakest of the Barbary States, yet it took the navy four years to defeat it. The war strained the government's finances, requiring it to impose a tax on imports.[34] By the time the navy fought next, it had become even smaller, and its enemy was enormously more powerful. The result nearly was disastrous.

FOUR

A Precarious Neutrality Ends in a Second War against Britain, 1805–1815

I

While almost the entire American navy was engaged in a war against Tripoli, the United States undertook crucial negotiations with France. In spite of their recent defeats in the war against Britain, France and its ally Spain still were the world's second and third largest naval powers. The United States was fortunate that it escaped a confrontation with one or both of them.

Immediately upon signing a truce with Britain on 1 October 1801, Napoleon Bonaparte, the first consul of the French republic, began outfitting a fleet to reestablish French control over St. Domingue and reintroduce slavery. He soon also began assembling a fleet to convoy 3,000 troops to Louisiana, which secretly had been promised to France by the king of Spain in exchange for territory in Italy for his son-in-law, Prince Louis of Parma. This exchange would leave France with the expense of administering Louisiana, previously valuable to Spain mostly as a buffer to protect Mexico from the United States. Louisiana was seen by Napoleon as a source of provisions for St. Domingue.

President Jefferson was warned by diplomats in Europe of

the impending French acquisition of Louisiana. This altered his policy toward France. He had led Napoleon to think that he would assist France in recovering St. Domingue, which Toussaint Louverture (with some assistance from John Adams) had made virtually independent. In spite of his hatred of a country ruled by former slaves, Jefferson now pulled back from providing provisions to the French army in St. Domingue. He also sent warnings to France that the United States would make an alliance with Britain should the French occupy Louisiana. His warnings were at first ignored as Napoleon realized that Britain was reluctant to contemplate a new war with France. The United States had no naval forces to prevent the French from sending troops to Louisiana. Meanwhile a huge French and Spanish fleet was involved in supporting the French army in St. Domingue.[1]

The crisis fortunately did not lead to renewed hostilities with France. The Senate narrowly defeated a series of resolutions that would have led to a preemptive American occupation of Louisiana, but Jefferson was ready to take action if negotiations with France failed. Luckily, Napoleon decided in April 1803 to sell Louisiana to the United States. The threat of war doubtless played a part, but several other factors also were important. His fleet and troops for Louisiana had not left Europe yet, partly due to Spanish slowness in providing France with the necessary authorization and partly due to logistical factors. Meanwhile the attempted French occupation of St. Domingue was foiled by disease and by the courageous resistance of Toussaint Louverture's army, even though its leader was captured. The massive loss of French lives convinced Napoleon that the war was hopeless. Without St. Domingue there was much less of a reason for keeping Louisiana. Perhaps most crucial were indications that the brief peace with Britain would soon end. The British feared French expansion in Europe and refused to evacuate the strategically important island of Malta as was called for in the recent Franco-British final peace treaty; Napoleon considered this a cause for war. In desperate need of money to fight a new war and realizing that Britain could easily occupy Louisiana, he decided to sell it to the United States while France was still at peace. He signed a treaty with the diplomats Robert Livingston and James Monroe on 2 May 1803, only sixteen days before Britain declared war on France.

The greatest threat of a war with the United States came from Spain rather than France. Charles IV of Spain was outraged at Napoleon's breaking his promise not to transfer Louisiana to another country. To prevent America from acquiring Louisiana, the Spanish government alerted its fleet in Havana to prepare to blockade American ports. The American representative in Spain in turn threatened to use the tiny fleet in the Mediterranean against the Spaniards and their huge navy. Fortunately, the impending crisis in Europe caused the Spaniards to reconsider.[2] In spite of the lack of American naval power, Louisiana was transferred to the United States a few weeks after Spanish officials transferred it to France. The United States acquired Louisiana for $15 million. Britain did nothing to block the sale, and a British bank even arranged the initial installment of the payment soon after the outbreak of Britain's war with France.

II

This new war put the United States in the same position as during the Franco-British war of 1793–1801. Jefferson was eager to trade with both of the combatants while maintaining neutrality. Neither France nor Britain wanted America to trade with its enemy. As the war continued, both powers resorted to economic warfare, including interference with American trade.[3] Moreover the British believed that the manpower needs of its navy required it to seize sailors of suspected British birth from American ships. At least 6,000 seamen were removed from ships between 1803 and 1812, more than twice the number that had been taken between 1793 and 1802.[4] This practice, called impressment, also became a key cause of the deterioration of American relations with Britain.

The U.S. government responded to the seizure of its ships and seamen by attempting to put economic pressure on Britain and France. Jefferson and his key advisor, Treasury Secretary Albert Gallatin, believed that the American navy was overly expensive but still too weak for a war and that building frigates or ships of the line would be too provocative to Britain. Their policy continued when James Madison assumed the presidency in 1809. In early 1812 Congress rejected a proposal for constructing ten more frigates. Consequently the largest American warships commissioned between 1800 and 1812 were the brigs *Hornet*, 18, *Wasp*, 18, *Argus*, 16, and *Syren* (later *Siren*), 16.[5] Instead, the U.S. government built small gunboats carrying 1–3 cannon like those used to defend Philadelphia in 1777. The gunboats had both sails and sweeps (oars) and were designed for harbor defense; substantial sums also were spent on harbor fortifications, which like gunboats were considered to pose little danger to republican institutions or the maintenance of peace. In 1803 Congress authorized the building of 15 gunboats. Another 25 were authorized in 1805, 50 more in 1806, and 188 more in 1807. A few were used at

Tripoli, whose defenders also used gunboats. Although individual gunboats were inexpensive, they were too fragile for rough seas; when war broke out in 1812, there were barely 60 left in service.[6]

Not only were no new frigates built, but those returning from the Mediterranean were taken out of service. By the beginning of 1807 only the *Constitution*, serving in the Mediterranean, was still at sea. In January 1807 Secretary of the Navy Robert Smith ordered the *Chesapeake*, 36, back in service in order to relieve the *Constitution*. In assembling a crew, it took aboard several deserters from British warships stationed off the east coast. Just after departing for the Mediterranean on 22 June 1807, it encountered a British squadron off Cape Henry. One of the ships, the *Leopard*, 50, came alongside to demand permission to search the *Chesapeake* for British deserters. When this was refused, the *Leopard* attacked the American ship, which was unprepared for combat. After suffering some twenty casualties, the *Chesapeake* surrendered, upon which the British searched the ship for deserters and removed four men.[7]

Jefferson compared the incident to the attack on the minutemen of Concord and Lexington. Americans were ready to go to war over the incident, but Jefferson hesitated because thousands of vulnerable merchant ships were at sea. The war fever soon abated. Jefferson, who was ready for a real war, had to settle for a trade war.[8] He cut off trade not only with Britain and France but with all of Europe and its colonies. This embargo did huge damage to American trade and particularly outraged New Englanders who, more than other Americans, depended on foreign trade for their livelihood. The navy was too weak to prevent smuggling, and Britain was able to find other markets and sources of raw materials such as U.S. naval supplies. Particularly important to the British navy was the development of Canada as an alternative source of timber.[9] The embargo was replaced in early 1809 with trade restrictions only on Britain and France and then in 1810 with the end of trade restrictions; in 1809 Congress voted that four frigates should be added to the two currently in service. Britain continued to seize ships that were trying to trade with France without a British license, while France seized ships that had accepted a British license. America threatened to reinstate trade restrictions on one of them if the other promised to end its hostile practices. Napoleon quickly seized the opportunity, falsely announcing the end of restrictions on American ships. Although French prize courts continued to impound American ships, President Madison was glad for an excuse to restore sanctions on Britain, a miscalculation that eventually helped lead to war.

Ironically, this time the sanctions had an effect. Britain, suffering from a severe economic depression, finally withdrew its restrictions on American trade in June 1812. It was too late. Earlier that month Madison, despairing of peaceful methods, had requested and received from Congress a declaration of war against the British. He hoped that by seizing Canada the United States could force the British to end impressment and discriminatory trade practices. (Settlers in the American West also blamed the British for an Indian war that recently had begun in Indiana, and they wished to keep Canada for their own protection.)[10] Madison hoped for a limited war ending in a nearly bloodless victory in Canada; although Americans hoped to profit from Napoleon's anticipated continued victories,[11] they had little sympathy for France and no desire to undo the Convention of Mortfontaine, by which America had declared its independence from European alliances and power politics. Some even wished to declare war on France as well as Britain, and for the first year of the war American merchants continued selling grain to the British army that was fighting the French in Spain.

Madison also hoped to pressure the British by seizing their merchant ships, but he put his faith chiefly in privateers. When war was declared, the American navy had only five frigates ready for use (*Constitution*, 44, *President*, 44, *United States*, 44, *Congress*, 36, and *Essex*, 32). Congress had just approved returning several other frigates to service, and eventually the *Chesapeake*, 36, *Constellation*, 36, and *John Adams*, 28, rejoined the navy, but the *Adams* was reduced to a sloop of war and the *New York*, *Boston*, and *General Greene* were beyond repair.[12] The navy had fewer frigates available than when it had fought the French in the West Indies or when it had fought the corsairs of Tripoli. Moreover its enemy was far more dangerous. Britain's navy was the most powerful in the history of the world, having 110 ships of the line, 4 50-gun ships, and 134 frigates in service.[13]

III

American plans for a quick occupation of Canada quickly proved unrealistic.[14] As in 1775, Canadians did not welcome an American invasion. The American army was untrained and unprepared for the logistical difficulties it faced. All its attempts against Canada failed.

Its major thrust was in the area between Lake Erie and Lake Huron. An American army marched from central Ohio to Detroit and then across the Detroit River into Upper Canada. The threat of a British counterattack forced it to retreat, after which the British captured Detroit and most of the American army. Meanwhile the British also captured Fort Dearborn, near the site of today's Chicago, as well as Mackinac Island in the northern part of Lake Huron.

Two other American offensives also failed. A small American force crossed the Niagara River, but it too was captured. Another American force, following the traditional Lake Champlain route toward Montreal, retreated without a battle.

Americans generally were less optimistic about the prospects of their navy, particularly since the British fleet at Halifax (a ship of the line, half a dozen frigates, and sixteen smaller ships) was more powerful than the entire American navy.[15] For several reasons, however, the Americans did surprisingly well during the opening year of the war. The British were slow to begin hostilities, hoping that their repeal of trade restrictions against the United States would bring the war to a quick conclusion without their having to divert resources from the fight against Napoleon. In contrast to the army, the American navy, although very small, was of high quality. Because it was so small, there was an adequate supply of officers and sailors, and its ships were well constructed. Although its ship captains had little experience of sailing in a line of battle, they had been well trained by serving with excellent officers like Truxtun and Preble. They quickly proved adept at single ship combat.[16]

On 21 June 1812, just three days after Congress declared war on Great Britain, Commodore John Rodgers sailed from Boston with a squadron of five ships (*President*, 44, *United States*, 44, *Congress*, 36, *Hornet*, 18, and *Argus*, 16) in the hope of intercepting a rich convoy from Jamaica. In early July the *Essex*, 32, sailed from New York and the *Constitution*, 44, from Annapolis in the vain hope of joining Rodgers at sea.

The Jamaica convoy escaped, but Rodger's squadron, sailing across the Atlantic, so disconcerted the British that hundreds of American merchant ships returning home escaped capture. (A French squadron in 1755 had foiled the British in a similar manner, although less thoroughly.)[17] Vice Admiral Herbert Sawyer's Halifax fleet sailed to the area of New York, but it did not have enough ships to gain control of American waters. It came close to intercepting the *Constitution*, but the American frigate escaped to Boston and then returned to sea and captured one of Sawyer's frigates, the *Guerriere*, 38. All of the other American frigates also returned to port safely.

With the British now alerted, it had become too dangerous for most of the American navy to sail together, so it was decided that henceforth no more than two frigates and one smaller ship should sail in company. In October 1812 all five of the American frigates sailed again, joined in December by a sixth, the *Chesapeake*, 36. These cruises, too, were successful. Two more British frigates were captured (the *Java*, 38, by the *Constitution*, and the *Macedonian*, 38, by the *United States*), while the *Essex* rounded Cape Horn and undertook a cruise in the Pacific that lasted until it was captured in 1814; one of the prizes, the *Macedonian*, was repaired, brought safely to New York, and added to the American navy. British naval officers and the British public were badly shaken by the capture of the three frigates, although their loss had little strategic importance. Naval officers, prone to dueling among themselves, tended to treat single ship combat as a duel and felt Britain had been dishonored by defeat; the public felt defeat as a blow to its pride, much as the public reacts today to unwelcome results of sporting events. Conversely the successful American naval captains, Isaac Hull and William Bainbridge of the *Constitution* and Stephen Decatur of the *United States*, raised morale and became national heroes. All three captains handled their ships well, but in every case the British were heavily outgunned, carrying 18-pounders against American 24-pounders.[18]

The American victories carried the seeds of defeat. American warships captured no more British frigates after 1812, as the British quickly poured reinforcements into North American waters. By early 1813 the British had a dozen ships of the line, thirty-eight frigates, and fifty-two smaller warships on the North American station.[19] Gradually the British blockaded the American coast: Chesapeake and Delaware Bays in February 1813, the entire American coast south of Long Island Sound in November 1813, and finally the New England coast (spared previously because of its extensive illicit trade with Canada) in April 1814.[20] The *United States, Macedonian,* and newly repaired *Constellation* were trapped in port by British blockading squadrons for the remainder of the war, and the *Chesapeake* was captured in June 1813 by a British frigate, leaving the *Constitution, Congress, President, Essex,* and *John Adams* as the last available American frigates.

Fortunately the American navy was able to adjust its strategy to the new realities. On 31 December 1812, Paul Hamilton, the ineffectual American secretary of the navy, resigned his office. His replacement was William Jones, a shipowner who, in addition to military service, had served on a privateer during the American Revolution. Jones proved an excellent choice, as Stoddert had been during the Quasi-War.[21] He used whatever warships could escape the British blockade to raid British shipping, thereby drawing British warships away from the American coast. About twenty naval warships made it to sea during the war (exclusive of gunboats that took few prizes). Due to their large size, they were an excellent addition to the some 500 privateers that cruised against British shipping.[22] Because of the need to protect their own trade, the British blockade never had enough ships on station to be completely effective even though it greatly reduced American trade.[23]

The second aspect of Jones's strategy was the high priority it placed on inland waters. American warships stranded in port such as the *Macedonian, John Adams,* and *Constitution* were used to provide crews for warships being built on the Great Lakes; by the end of 1814 almost a third of the navy's 10,700 crewmen were serving aboard fresh water ships. Jones wrote Isaac Chauncey, commodore of the squadron on Lake Ontario, that it was impossible to overestimate the importance of naval operations on the lakes. He demonstrated his commitment by paying the crewmen of idle ships a bonus to transfer to the lake squadrons.[24]

In spite of the fame of their seagoing colleagues, the most crucial naval officers during the war were the talented commanders of the lake squadrons: Chauncey, whose squadron was by far the largest, Captain Oliver Hazard Perry on Lake Erie, and Master Commandant Thomas Macdonough on Lake Champlain. Chauncey, a superb administrator, participated in the navy's biggest actions involving competing lines of battle, particularly the so-called Burlington Races of 28 September 1813. He faced an excellent opponent in Commodore Sir James Lucas Yeo, however, and was not able to win a decisive battle. A building race ensued; by war's end Yeo had a ship of the line, the *St. Lawrence,* 102, in service, and both the Americans and British had other ships of the line under construction.[25]

The key battle in 1813, however, was fought on Lake Erie.

Success was based on which side could assemble supplies and shipwrights to build the larger squadron and could find sailors to man it. The Americans had the advantage of shorter supply lines. Their dockyard at Presque Isle (Erie) at the southeast corner of Lake Erie was close to Pittsburgh, whereas the British dockyard at Amherstburg at the northwest tip of Lake Erie was a long distance from the nearest major British base, York (Toronto) on Lake Ontario. Moreover, Chauncey was able to provide more crewmen for the American squadron than could Yeo for the British. When Perry sailed in search of the enemy in August, he had nine ships carrying 64 cannon and 532 officers and crewmen. Commander Robert Barclay's rival squadron had six ships carrying 63 cannon and 440 officers and crewmen. The Battle of Lake Erie, fought on 10 September 1813, nearly was a British victory, however. Master Commandant Jesse Elliott, commanding the *Niagara*, 20, rigidly followed Perry's orders to maintain the line of battle, leaving the brunt of the battle to Perry's flagship, the *Lawrence*, 20. Perry transferred to the *Niagara* in the middle of the battle, however, and brought it into close action. As a result, the entire British fleet was captured.[26] The Americans were then able to recapture Detroit and to capture Amherstburg without a fight. They pursued the retreating British army, catching and defeating it at the Thames River, where the great Indian leader Tecumseh, a key British ally, was killed.[27] For reasons of logistics the Americans could not follow up the victory. Meanwhile, fighting along the strategically vital Niagara River frontier ended in stalemate.

The main threat to the United States in 1813 came from a large fleet sent to Chesapeake Bay by Vice Admiral Sir John Borlase Warren, the new commander of the North American station. Although the fleet operated in the bay from March to September 1813, using more than half of Warren's ships, its numerous raids ashore accomplished little; even the *Constellation*, trapped near Norfolk, escaped capture.[28]

Warren was replaced for the 1814 campaign by Vice Admiral Alexander Cochrane, who extended the blockade to New England. Again the British used a large proportion of their ships in Chesapeake Bay. When a British landing party captured Washington, the commandant of the naval shipyard ordered it burned. A frigate under construction and a newly launched sloop of war thus were destroyed to avoid their capture by British ships in the Potomac. Three weeks later the British bombarded Baltimore, but its defenses proved too strong for a landing party. Outside of Chesapeake Bay, though, they did not have enough ships to cut off American trade and privateering, even though most American naval warships were trapped in port.[29]

Elsewhere the main threat now came from the British army. With the defeat of Napoleon, the British were free to send a large body of reinforcements to Canada. British troops captured much of the coast of Maine, and a body of some 10,000 men marched to Plattsburgh on Lake Champlain. Their attack on the town was abandoned, however, when the supporting British squadron on Lake Champlain was destroyed by Macdonough's rival squadron. The British army was too large to be supplied by land and thus had to return to Canada.[30]

Macdonough's brilliant victory destroyed British hopes of adjusting the border between Canada and the United States. Fearful of new difficulties in Europe, they were willing to settle for a peace based on a return to prewar conditions, while leaving unresolved issues like impressment. An excellent American negotiating team (John Quincy Adams, Henry Clay, Albert Gallatin, James A. Bayard, and Jonathan Russell) negotiated a treaty on those terms with a British delegation in the neutral city of Ghent in today's Belgium; Clay and Russell had come to Europe on the *John Adams*, the only American frigate active during nearly all of the second half of 1814. The treaty was signed on 24 December 1814.[31]

Before news of peace could reach America, there were several more naval actions, including the capture of the *President* by a British squadron on 15 January 1815 and the *Constitution*'s capture of the *Cyane*, 22, and *Levant*, 20, on 20 February 1815. There was also a major battle on land, the repulse of a British raid on New Orleans on 8 January 1815. It is unlikely that a British victory would have led to a renegotiation of the peace treaty; the American triumph, however, bolstered self-confidence and helped Andrew Jackson, the commanding American general, rise to national prominence.[32]

IV

How did the United States survive intact in spite of its navy being virtually driven from the sea? Its navy had been virtually annihilated during the War of American Independence, but the French, Dutch, and Spanish navies had borne the brunt of the fighting. During the War of 1812 the United States insisted on fighting the British without French help. (The French did allow American privateers the use of their ports, a privilege not reciprocated by the United States.)[33]

An important factor in America's survival was the advantage of being on the defensive, the same advantage that helped Canada survive American attack. Moreover, the War of 1812 was a throwback to the limited wars of the eighteenth century, fought by small armies for relatively narrow objectives. Such conflicts usually were wars of attrition, ended when the parties to the war decided it was no longer worth the expense. In such cases the side with the most to lose sometimes could prevail by refusing to accept defeat, as France did in 1762, achieving a peace in which it saved its vital interests.[34] Similarly the United States was able to recoup its losses such as Mackinac Island and the coast of Maine by refusing to accept their loss; peace was more important to Britain than was achieving minor gains along the Canadian border.

Although the American navy was largely confined to port by war's end, it played an important part in stalemating the British war effort. Secretary of the Navy Jones's strategy of using the navy to attack British commerce in order to divert British naval strength while giving priority to American naval forces on Lake Ontario, Lake Erie, and Lake Champlain proved surprisingly successful.[35] Denied victory along the northern border of the United States, the British were forced to resort to raids, such as the one on Washington, but these were insufficient to break American will. British exhaustion from the long war against France prevented them from pursuing the strategy that had almost succeeded during the War of American Independence, applying pressure on the American economy until it was ruined and the American government was bankrupt.

Nonetheless the war revealed that the United States had made only limited progress in overcoming its colonial heritage. The navy lacked the infrastructure and industrial base to support more than a tiny navy by European standards; not until 1833, for example, did it have a dry dock in which to repair ships.[36] Its administrative structure also was primitive, although at the end of the war it adopted Jones's suggestion of establishing a board of naval commissioners to advise the secretary of the navy; the first commissioners were war heroes: Captains Isaac Hull, John Rodgers, and David Porter (former captain of the *Essex*), followed by Stephen Decatur when Hull resigned.[37] Thanks to the navy's accomplishments, there was no danger that it would fade away as it had after the end of the War of American Independence. But its support was limited and varied according to proximity to the coastline and interest in foreign trade. Americans living west of the Appalachian Mountains continued to resist spending money on an oceanic fleet. (It is no coincidence that during the war the navy had its greatest success on inland waters near the frontier.) The government lacked the financial resources to pay for an extended war and was approaching economic disaster by war's end. The executive branch of government was still weak, while Congress was divided and faction ridden. Thus the government was unable to raise the taxes necessary to support an adequate army and navy. Perhaps most seriously the United States still was largely a collection of states rather than a unified country. During the war the New England states had traded with the enemy, given little cooperation to the American war effort, and near war's end they even made a token threat to secede.[38]

The War of 1812 was a near disaster. In the short run it stimulated naval construction in order to respond more effectively to a similar threat in the future. As the danger of a new European war receded, however, this growth slowed. For the next forty-five years the navy was large enough to protect American commerce from pirates and to intimidate less advanced countries with small navies or none. It was not large or modern enough, though, to fight a serious naval power like Britain, France, or Russia. Hence the United States had to adopt a cautious and moderate foreign policy where Europe was concerned.

FIVE

Trade Protection and War with Mexico, 1815–1861

I

The United States attempted with only limited success to expand its navy during the War of 1812. Between 1813 and the end of 1815 it launched the 74-gun ships of the line *Independence, Washington,* and *Franklin,* the 44-gun frigates *Guerriere* and *Java* (a sister ship, the *Essex,* was destroyed before launching when the British captured Washington), and the 18-gun sloops *Erie, Ontario, Frolic, Peacock,* and *Wasp* (while a sixth sloop also was destroyed at Washington).[1] Of these ships only the *Frolic, Peacock,* and *Wasp* were able to sail before war's end. Shortly thereafter, however, some of the new ships were given an opportunity to prove their worth. During 1814 and 1815 the Barbary States, seeing that their commercial opportunities in the Mediterranean were declining due to the end of the Napoleonic War, reverted to armed attacks on neutral shipping. On 23 February 1815 the United States declared war on Algiers, the most powerful and aggressive of the Barbary States. It fitted out a fleet including the ship of the line *Independence* and five frigates and assigned Commodore William Bainbridge as its commander.

As preparing so large a fleet was time-consuming, Stephen Decatur was sent ahead with an advanced squadron consisting of the frigates *Guerriere, Macedonian,* and *Constellation,* as well as seven smaller vessels. Decatur's squadron captured an Algerian frigate, forced the Algerians to make peace, and reestablished relations with Tunis and Tripoli before the rest of the fleet reached the Mediterranean.[2] The threat from the Barbary States did not end, however. A squadron was left in the Mediterranean to protect U.S. trade. Although a large British fleet bombarded Algiers in 1816, suffering heavy casualties in the process, the menace was not brought completely under control until the French occupied Algiers in 1830.[3]

With the United States now at peace, Congress moved to prevent an eventual repetition of the 1812–14 war during which the navy had been too small to protect shipping or even the east coast from the British. On 19 April 1816 Congress approved spending $8 million over the next eight years in order to build nine more ships of the line of 74 or more guns and twelve frigates of at least 44 guns (including a 74 and three 44's authorized in 1813). By the end of 1826 the navy had completed or at least begun work on nine ships of the line, ten 44-gun frigates, and half a dozen 18-gun sloops. This building program, the largest before the Civil War, proved far too ambitious. There were not enough funds to finish all the ships or enough sailors to man them. The *Columbus, 74, North Carolina, 74, Delaware, 74,* and *Ohio, 74,* were launched in 1819–20 and the *Pennsylvania, 120,* in 1837, but work was suspended on four other 74's pending a need for them; all of the frigates eventually were completed, but only four of them were launched by 1830.

The navy could not even use all the ships that were launched.

Although the ships of the line impressed the British with the size of their cannon, they were unsatisfactory in other ways. Only the *Ohio* had a good reputation for her sailing qualities, and the three ships of the line launched by 1815 were unable to make much use of their full armament because their lower gun ports were too close to the waterline; the *Washington* and *Franklin* were quickly taken out of service, and the *Independence* eventually was converted to a 54-gun frigate. Each year from 1816 to 1851 there were between one and three ships of the line in service, but only the *Ohio* and *Delaware* were used for more than ten years. The massive *Pennsylvania*, one of the largest ships of the line in the world, was obsolete by the time it finally was launched. It sailed from Philadelphia to Norfolk and was promptly taken out of service.[4]

Abel Upshur, arguably the best secretary of the navy during the period, argued that the navy needed to be half as strong as the British in order to act as a deterrent. It never came close. Between 1815 and 1850 the British never had fewer than fifty ships of the line in service or reserve; of these at least a dozen were in commission during every year except 1844 and 1845.[5] The American navy was able to intimidate the Kingdom of the Two Sicilies (formerly the kingdoms of Naples and Sicily) into signing a commercial treaty in 1832,[6] but it was substantially smaller than not only the British navy but also the navies of France (with twenty-four to thirty-eight ships of the line between 1820 and 1850) and Russia (with forty-three to forty-seven ships of the line).[7] Britain did not ignore the United States as a possible threat, but this was chiefly out of concern for Canada and because it feared that the United States might form a new alliance with France. The great naval expansion program of 1816 thus was only of limited value.

II

There were a number of reasons for the failure of the United States to build a navy that adequately reflected its growing population and economic development.[8] One was the gradual reduction of the risk of a new war with Britain. Faced with a huge national debt and social unrest after the end of the Napoleonic War, the British government was anxious for better relations with the United States. The British, although chronically short of sailors, abandoned impressment.[9] The issue of neutral shipping rights became academic, and the British betrayal of their Indian allies on the American frontier greatly diminished tension with the United States. Of great importance, too, was the caution and good sense of one of the greatest foreign secretaries in British history, Robert Stewart, Viscount Castlereagh. Having approved the Treaty of Ghent, Castlereagh devoted his enormous skills to preventing a new war in spite of such provocations as General Andrew Jackson's judicial murder of two British citizens during his 1818 incursion into Spanish East Florida.[10] During his tenure in office, the United States and Britain signed the Rush-Bagot agreement of 1817, severely limiting the size of naval forces on the Great Lakes, and the Convention of 1818, delineating the Canadian-American border between the Great Lakes and the Rocky Mountains, while postponing a decision on ownership of the Oregon territory.[11] The United States then signed the 1819 Transcontinental Treaty with Spain, by which the United States acquired all of Florida and delineated Spanish Mexico's borders with Oregon and Louisiana. Although the navy played a role in the preceding American incursions into Florida, Spain was more influenced by the indefensibility of the portions of Florida that it still held, its own internal problems, and the crippling of its navy during the wars of 1792–1814.[12]

Spain's empire in the Western Hemisphere soon was torn by revolt. In 1823 George Canning, who had succeeded Castlereagh the previous year, suggested to the United States a joint statement disavowing their interest in acquiring Spanish territory and warning other European powers not to intervene in the Western Hemisphere. The United States declined the offer, not wishing to be prevented from acquiring former Spanish territory itself. Instead President James Monroe issued a statement warning all European nations against attempting to acquire new colonies in the Western Hemisphere; in return the United States would not interfere with existing colonies or intervene in European disputes. The Monroe Doctrine was more important as a precedent for future American policy than it was for its immediate impact. It was the British navy that protected Latin America (rapidly becoming a British economic satellite); moreover, the other European powers were not interested in becoming involved in disputes outside their own continent.[13] Symbolically, however, the rejection of British help in defending the Americas was of great importance. It both proclaimed the entire mainland of the Western Hemisphere south of Canada as an American sphere of influence and served as a final declaration of independence from the European balance of power, a policy first articulated by Thomas Paine in 1776, but implicit in the goals of the first settlers of New England 150 years earlier. The narrow escape in the War of 1812 helped give Americans the confidence to complete the fifty-year-long process of emancipation from Europe and its wars, an important step in America's overcoming its colonial legacy. It, however, had yet to complete the process by achieving economic self-sufficiency, political maturity, and national unity.

Relations with Britain continued to improve in spite of ir-
ritants like Britain's denying American trade full access to
British West Indies. Great Britain and the United States became each other's best customers and, to Britain's surprise,
even President Andrew Jackson proved cooperative and reasonable (the British being too strong to bully).[14] One of the
most important issues, the border between Maine and Canada, was resolved in 1842 by a compromise. This was facili-
tated both by American fears of the British navy and by the
good fortune that the American secretary of state, Daniel Web-
ster, was an Anglophile, while the British secretary of state,
the Earl of Aberdeen, was a man of exceptional honor and de-
cency.[15] This left Oregon as the major outstanding issue between Britain and the United States. Meanwhile, American
disputes with other European states were less dangerous, as
they chiefly involved commercial rights and financial claims
stemming from the Napoleonic Wars. There was a war scare
involving France during the Jackson administration, but as
it was motivated mostly by politics and national pride, it was
less dangerous than it appeared.[16]

With no obvious threat to meet, congressional support for
large naval expenditures waned by the early 1820s. Although
John Quincy Adams was a supporter of the navy and Andrew
Jackson eventually became one, power over appropriations
rested with Congress, which questioned the value of completing or keeping in service ships of the line just to show the flag.
Moreover sectional and political rivalries proved impossible to
overcome. Although easterners and Whigs generally favored
a strong navy, westerners and Democrats were more interested in keeping government expenses low. Thus most of the
navy's large ships were kept "in ordinary" (left unmanned).[17]

Throughout the 1820s and 1830s the navy also suffered from weak leadership. Naval secretaries were selected for political reasons and, not surprisingly, usually accomplished little.[18] The Board of Naval Commissioners, originally intended as a reform measure, became increasingly conservative, particularly regarding technological change. In 1814 the navy had launched a steam warship designed by Robert Fulton that he wished to call the *Demologus,* but which was named *Fulton* after his death in 1815. Although designed as a floating battery for the protection of New York Harbor, this paddlewheel driven vessel was powerfully armed and could attain a respectable speed of six knots. It was only used, however, as a receiving ship for new sailors. In 1829 it was destroyed when its gunpowder magazine exploded. It was not replaced until 1837, when a second ship called the *Fulton* was placed in commission. In contrast, the British navy had forty steam-powered vessels by 1840.[19] Dominated by veterans of the War of 1812, the Board of Naval Commissioners was still thinking in terms of the last war, not future conflicts. Progress had to come from younger officers.

III

For the three decades following the War of 1812, the navy did not have an enemy, but it did have a mission—the protection of American commerce and citizens.[20] It was to protect shipping from Barbary corsairs that the Mediterranean squadron was established in 1815. Even after the elimination of the Barbary States as a threat, a squadron was needed in the Mediterranean to show the flag and protect shipping. During the Greek war of independence in the 1820s, for example, pirates and privateers lurked in the Aegean Sea. During the long wars that established new states from Mexico to Argentina, Spanish privateers from Cuba and rebel privateers from the mainland began seizing American and other neutral ships. To protect shipping, a West India squadron and a Pacific squadron were established in the early 1820s and a Brazil squadron in 1826.[21] Slave traders were treated as pirates, too, but American efforts at catching them were generally unsuccessful, as they had to be captured flying an American flag. The navy even established an African squadron in 1843 to work with the British in suppressing the slave trade, but in general it was more concerned with preventing British ships from searching American ships than it was with capturing slave ships; not until 1859 were any steam-powered ships assigned to it.[22]

In addition to protecting ships from pirates, the navy performed a number of other services, from rescuing shipwrecked sailors to producing nautical charts in order to prevent shipwrecks. In 1830 the navy established a Department of Charts and Instruments, the forerunner of the U.S. Naval Observatory; between 1838 and 1842 Charles Wilkes's U.S. Exploring Expedition made extensive surveys of various island chains in the Pacific (while also reconnoitering the coasts of Oregon and Mexican California).[23] More problematical were acts of retribution for harm done to American ships or citizens. Naval captains sometimes went beyond their orders. When the Argentine governor of the Falkland Islands seized three American schooners in 1831, the sloop *Lexington* captured the islands.[24] Eleven years later Commodore Thomas ap Catesby Jones of the Pacific squadron heard rumors that war had broken out with Mexico. Perhaps acting on prior advice of Upshur or President John Tyler, he brought the frigate *United States* to Monterey, the capital of California, and seized the city. He

quickly learned the rumor was false and departed after apol-
ogizing.[25] The most appalling incident involved Captain John
Downes of the frigate *Potomac*, who in 1832 burned the village
of Quallah Battoo in Sumatra in retribution for the murder
a year earlier of an American captain and two sailors. More
than 100 natives were killed; there is no indication any of them
were involved in the murders.[26] The navy during this age of
"Manifest Destiny" reflected the aggressive, self-righteous,
and racist side of the colonial legacy that independence had
done little to check; compared, however, with the British or
French, it was relatively restrained in the use of force against
non-Europeans.

With the expansion of American trade, the navy's responsi-
bilities grew. An East India squadron was established in 1835,
and the navy soon was involved in establishing the right of
American ships to use specified ports in China.[27] These re-
sponsibilities often involved long and arduous cruises. Although not having to face combat, sailors had no chance for
prize money and often had to endure a difficult life.

IV

American ships and shipboard life did not differ greatly from
those in the British and French navies. Much depended on
where the ship was stationed (the Mediterranean being particularly appealing) and the character of its captain. As in
other navies, captains might be feared, respected, or beloved;
among other examples Isaac Hull and Stephen Decatur were
loved by their crews, while Captains Isaac McKeever of the *Independence* and Thomas Gedney of the sloop *Plymouth* were
known for their kindness. One of the most popular captains
was the eccentric "Mad Jack" Percival, who, like his friend

Hull, took particular pains to train his midshipmen and who was renowned for his seamanship and concern for his sailors; among the midshipman he trained was Gustavus Vasa Fox, who became assistant secretary of the navy during the Civil War. Many captains like Matthew Calbraith Perry, however, followed the precepts of Commodore John Rodgers, famous for his unrelenting discipline, and treated their crews harshly.[28]

Bad treatment of crews was caused partly by officers' frustration. Officers in general had limited career opportunities. Promotions were strictly by seniority and were slowed by the presence of numerous elderly or incompetent officers who could not be removed. Moreover, the highest rank in the navy was that of captain because Congress repeatedly refused to approve the appointment of admirals.[29]

Discipline was harsh also because crews were uneven in quality. With ample chances for service in an expanding merchant marine or for acquiring land, it was difficult to find good crews. Moreover, the U.S. navy depended on volunteers who signed up for a limited time. Prior to 1820, tours of duty were no longer than two years (American warships sailing no further than the Mediterranean), and after that they were no longer than three. This had a major effect on American naval operations. For example, after sailing around the world, the *Constitution* had to leave Mexican waters on the eve of the American-Mexican war, in order to return its crew to Boston.[30] Because crews had to be reconstructed so often, ships generally began cruises with a large number of untrained and undisciplined men, many of them foreigners in spite of its being illegal to employ them. Unlike the army, the navy used free blacks (and even some slaves) and hence did not have the new challenge of integration to face when the Civil War demanded an unprecedented number of men.

The difficult conditions faced by American sailors, however, form only half the story. Although it was common to compare a warship to a prison, such ships had another side. American crews were better paid and better fed than their British counterparts, and between 1806 and 1862 they had the privilege of drinking American whiskey in their grog.[31] Their crews had camaraderie, a sense of humor, and pride. Herman Melville, who served a year on the *United States*, wrote of both the good and the bad in his 1850 novel, *White-Jacket*. Although it may exaggerate the brutality of shipboard life for the sake of telling a good story, it is an entertaining introduction to the navy of the 1840s. Melville particularly criticized the use of flogging (whipping) as a punishment; Congress abolished it in 1850.[32]

V

On 13 May 1846 the United States declared war on Mexico. The navy entered the war far better prepared than it had been a few years earlier, in large part due to the efforts of Abel Upshur, secretary of the navy from late 1841 to early 1843.[33] Upshur had managed to win a substantial increase in the naval budget; by the end of 1843 he had launched the frigates *Cumberland*, *Raritan*, and *Savannah*, the sloop *Saratoga*, the brigs *Bainbridge*, *Somers*, *Truxtun*, *Perry*, and *Lawrence*, the paddle steamers *Mississippi*, *Missouri*, and *Union*, the sidewheel gunboat *Michigan* (the first American warship built with an iron hull), and the revolutionary steamer *Princeton* (which replaced the paddlewheel with a screw propeller). Most would be used in the coming war.[34] Another innovation was the use of guns firing explosive shells; ironically, in 1844 Upshur, now secretary of state, was killed on a visit to the *Princeton* when one of its guns exploded.

Upshur's administrative changes were just as important. He persuaded Congress to replace the Board of Naval Commissioners with five bureaus, similar to the five departments established by the British in 1832 and the bureau system long used by the French navy. Each of the bureau chiefs reported directly to the secretary of the navy. Not only was the new system more efficient, but it ended the naval commissioners' ability to block innovation. Upshur also fought for the establishment of a naval academy, long advocated by supporters of reform like Matthew Perry and the great oceanographer Matthew Maury. This, however, had to await the appointment of the historian George Bancroft as secretary of the navy in 1845.[35]

Upshur's innovations came just as the thirty-year peace after the War of 1812 was ending. In May 1844 an American naval squadron anchored off Galveston, a strong indication that the United States was ready to intervene in the still-continuing war between Texas and Mexico.[36] Soon thereafter Texas was admitted to the United States. In August 1845 Commodore David Conner, the capable commander of the Gulf Coast squadron (called the Home Fleet), was sent secret orders to blockade the Mexican coast should the Mexicans send troops across the Rio Grande, which the United States claimed as Texas's southern border, or in case war was declared. Orders already had been sent to Commodore John D. Sloat, the commander of the Pacific squadron, to seize San Francisco and blockade the rest of the coast in case of war with Mexico; meanwhile the British sent the *America*, 50, from the British Pacific squadron to visit the coasts of California and Oregon.[37]

The possibility that the British would seize California added an element of complexity to negotiations with Mexico to prevent war. American relations with Britain were tense also because of the dispute over the fate of Oregon; Britain even sent a secret agent to reconnoiter American defenses.[38] The American navy was hardly prepared to fight the British, and a solution was ready at hand: partitioning Oregon along the same line of latitude (49 degrees north) as the American-Canadian border to the east of the Rockies, while letting Britain keep all of Vancouver Island and access to Puget Sound. For both countries the real obstacles to peace were national pride, suspicion, and domestic politics. Fortunately the reasonable Earl of Aberdeen was still British foreign secretary, and President James K. Polk, for all his aggressive expansionism, was not foolish enough to fight Great Britain without having a navy capable of doing so. In June 1846 the Senate approved a peace treaty on the terms proposed by Great Britain.[39]

The previous month the United States had declared war on Mexico for attacking troops sent to the Rio Grande. The Mexicans had virtually no navy with which to fight. Their only two modern warships, the steam-powered iron ships *Guadaloupe* and *Montezuma*, were repossessed by the British contractors that had built them; the Mexicans did not have the crews to man them or the money to pay for them.[40] American threats, moreover, prevented other countries from fitting out privateers under the Mexican flag. The main difficulties facing the navy were logistical, as the Home Fleet operating off the Mexican coast was dependent on the naval base at Pensacola for coal and supplies, while the navy's Pacific squadron was largely thrown on its own resources. The new steamers constructed by Upshur were invaluable, and the navy purchased or captured a number of small steamers and sailing ships to supplement the huge fleets it managed to assemble in the Pacific and Gulf of Mexico (including the ships of the line *Ohio* and *Columbus*). Sloat's Pacific squadron occupied Monterey and San Francisco without a fight; subsequently the British ship of the line *Collingwood*, 80, arrived in Monterey Bay but quickly departed without incident. Soon all of Old California was in American hands. Sloat then turned over the Pacific squadron to Commodore Robert Stockton. Unfortunately, Stockton was a bully; he and his army and Marine Corps associates ruled California in such a heavy-handed manner that they caused a revolt leading to the loss of southern California until American troops began arriving from New Mexico. In 1847 Stockton was relieved by the competent and conciliatory Commodore James Biddle; during the war the Pacific squadron had five different commanders.

Meanwhile Conner's Home Fleet in the Gulf of Mexico blockaded the east coast of Mexico, gradually occupying ports (although such occupations often were temporary, as disease and sometimes guerrilla attacks took their toll). In March 1847 it landed an army of 8,600 men near Vera Cruz, the major Mexican port on the Gulf of Mexico and then contributed cannon and sailors to the subsequent capture of the city. During the siege Conner was replaced by his energetic second-in-command, Matthew Perry. Led by the able Major General Winfield Scott, the American troops at Vera Cruz went on to capture Mexico City in September 1847. Although Mexican forces in both California and interior Mexico fought with valor, their artillery and military equipment were unequal to that of the Americans, and their navy was negligible. The war ended in early 1848 with the Americans acquiring not only Mexican consent to the Rio Grande as a border for Texas but also title to New Mexico and California.[41]

VI

The victory was more costly than initially realized. The addition of Texas as a slaveholding state aroused the suspicion and hostility of abolitionists. Their efforts to block the expansion of slavery into the other areas taken from Mexico in turn aroused the suspicion and hostility of slaveholders. After a dozen years of bitterness, eleven slaveholding states seceded from the Union. The navy would play a vital role in suppressing the rebellion.

The Mexican War was important in preparing the navy for its participation in the Civil War. The navy's three principal tasks were blockading the Mexican coast, conducting landing operations with the army, and moving from the coast via river into the Mexican interior. These were the same tasks it would face in the Civil War, although on the latter occasion it would face resistance from a small but dangerous enemy navy.

The Mexican War also had important consequences for the weapons with which the navy would fight. Hitherto the American navy had been a smaller version of the British navy, using squadrons of ships of the line and frigates around the world to protect its trade. From the 1840s to the early 1860s Great Britain and France converted their huge fleets of ships of the line from sail to steam; by 1860 the British navy had more than fifty steam-powered ships of the line and the French navy had almost forty.[42] The few American ships of the line were too aged to make the effort. They were taken out of service and a new shipbuilding program was begun, one producing ships too small for fighting the British, but just right for fighting the Confederacy. Ironically it was predominantly Southerners who lobbied for the new ships. They hoped to use them to make conquests in Cuba or Central America into which slavery could expand. (Efforts to do so were blocked; filibustering expeditions into Nicaragua were defeated, partly because of the American navy, while Cuba could not be taken without risking war with Britain.)[43] The most important new ships were the screw-driven steam frigates *Merrimack, Wabash, Minnesota, Colorado, Roanoke,* and *Niagara,* the screw-driven steam sloops *Hartford, Brooklyn, Lancaster, Pensacola, Richmond, Mohican, Iroquois, Wyoming, Dacotah, Narragansett, Seminole,* and *Pawnee,* and the sailing frigates *Sabine* and *Santee.* All of these ships were launched between 1855 and early 1860. Nevertheless in January 1860 the navy had only about fifty ships.[44]

Meanwhile the French navy had launched the *Gloire,* a wooden battleship clad with armor, and was building several more as well as the *Couronne,* a battleship with an iron hull, while the British navy was building the iron-hulled battleships *Warrior* and *Black Prince.* The use of explosive shells during the recently concluded Crimean War, in which France and Britain participated as allies, doomed the now hopelessly vulnerable wooden warship. The introduction of iron had been delayed for a few years by the initial failure of iron to resist shells, but the use of ironclad floating gun batteries in the Black Sea convinced the British and French that armored ships were viable. Except for the gunboat *Michigan* on Lake Erie and the never completed experimental "Stevens battery," the U.S. navy of 1860 was built of wood.[45] Furthermore, although recently it had purged more than 100 of its most infirm or incompetent officers, thus permitting a wave of long overdue new promotions, it was still tied to the system of promotion by strict order of seniority, a sharp contrast to practice before 1815.[46]

As the United States slid toward civil war, the navy resumed its role of protecting American trade. By now that role involved opening new markets as well as guarding old ones. Its most prestigious triumph was an 1854 treaty giving the United States access to ports in Japan, a treaty negotiated under the guns of an American squadron commanded by Commodore Matthew Perry.[47] Sadly, the American merchant marine, second in size only to Britain's, would soon become a victim of a catastrophic rise in insurance costs due to war, costs which its European competitors could avoid.

SIX

The Civil War, 1861–1865

I

The navy was caught unprepared when, in response to the election of Abraham Lincoln, the states of South Carolina, Mississippi, Florida, Alabama, Georgia, Louisiana, and Texas chose to leave the Union. In early February 1861, through a self-proclaimed "Congress," the first six states named themselves the Confederate States of America, adopted a constitution, and selected former secretary of war Jefferson Davis as their president. (Texas, awaiting the results of a referendum, did not join until the end of the month.) They had no navy of their own, but the American navy faced the challenge of blockading the rebels' coast; once the original members were joined by the coastal states of Virginia and North Carolina and the inland states of Tennessee and Arkansas, the Confederacy had some 3,500 miles of coastline. To meet this challenge, the navy had only thirty-nine warships in commission (including a dozen in the Home Fleet), 1,500 officers (a quarter of whom left the navy when war broke out), and 7,500 seamen.[1]

The army's problems were just as daunting. Although the states remaining in the Union had twice the population of those departing, the Confederacy had the great advantage of being on the defensive. It thereby had shorter supply lines, interior lines of communication, and, for the most part, the support of local civilians.

In spite of the obstacles, the North possessed a number of advantages, not all of them immediately obvious. Far more than the Union, the Confederacy inherited the colonial legacy that had for so long hindered the growth of the American army and navy: an underdeveloped economy overwhelmingly based on agriculture, a central government with inadequate funds, rivalry among its states, and a shortage of trained military and naval officers; it particularly lacked the merchant shipping, sailors, infrastructure, and public support necessary to establish an effective navy of its own. The North, in contrast, had the underpinnings of a formidable war economy, particularly when it came to the navy: a huge shipbuilding industry, one of the world's largest iron industries, and facilities for producing arms such as the new shell guns invented by John Dahlgren, commander of the Washington Navy Yard. Its population was far larger and its transportation system, particularly railroads, was far superior to the South's.[2] It had an established naval bureaucracy, soon headed by the shrewd and forceful Gideon Welles, a former chief of the Bureau of Provisions and Clothing. Welles was able to overcome the stranglehold that tradition and seniority had put on the navy. He created new ranks such as ensign, lieutenant commander, and rear admiral (first called "flag officer"); since rear admiral appointments were open to all senior officers without regard to seniority, even a mere commander like the ambitious David D. Porter could hope for command of a fleet.[3] The navy could draw on the merchant marine for officers and sailors to replace those who departed. Among the officers remaining from the old navy were such bold leaders as Porter, Andrew Foote, and David G. Farragut.⁴ After the departure of Southern congressmen, President Lincoln had a Congress with which he could work, even though the Union (i.e., the states remaining loyal) still was plagued by political, regional, and state rivalries. Finally, and perhaps most importantly, the Union had in Lincoln a tough, decisive, and politically astute war leader who vastly expanded the power of the presidency in numerous areas from education (establishing land grant colleges) to transportation (starting work on a transcontinental railroad) to taxation. Above all, he expanded the president's ability to make war.

In spite of the Confederacy's enormous size (comparable in area to the Union states), it had geographical weaknesses that the Union was able to exploit. Its huge coastline made it difficult to blockade but also difficult to defend. Because of its need to import war materiel and consumer goods, it had to protect its ports; moreover, powerful local politicians insisted that troops be allocated to defend them. Thus it could not devote its resources just to protecting its long northern border. The defense of ports like Charleston drained troops from its major armies. A second problem was the American river system, which helped the Union. Washington and the Midwest were protected by the Potomac and Ohio Rivers. Only one small army was ever able to approach Washington from the north (in 1864), and only tiny cavalry raids in 1862 and 1863 threatened the Midwest. Lacking naval strength, the Confederacy was unable to make much use of rivers for defensive purposes; for example, it could not prevent Union armies from fording eastward-flowing rivers like the Rappahannock that formed part of their defense system. Of even greater importance, the South was penetrated by the Mississippi River, flowing north to south, and the Tennessee and Cumberland Rivers, whose lower regions flowed south to north. By using these rivers the Union could strike deeply into the South and negate its interior lines of communication unless the South moved quickly to plug access by defensible forts and a strong river fleet. The Union's brown water or river navy hence proved as important as its blue water or ocean navy. During 1861 the Union navy began to construct both.

II

Although the Confederate states initially did not expect war, they were faced with the presence of small Union garrisons in several forts within their territory, including Fort Sumter in Charleston Harbor and Fort Pickens off Pensacola, Florida. The initial Confederate response was to take no action unless there was an attempt to reinforce them, hoping that the government in Washington eventually would evacuate them. Fort Sumter was the more vulnerable because it was surrounded by potentially hostile forts and because its supply of food was very limited. After an attempt to resupply it was turned back in January 1861, outgoing President James Buchanan took no further action, leaving the matter to the incoming president, Lincoln. In his 4 March 1861 inaugural address Lincoln pledged he would hold government property within the Southern states. He immediately learned that the garrison at Fort Sumter was running so low on food he would have to take quick action. His new secretary of state, William Henry Seward, favored evacuating Fort Sumter while reinforcing Fort Pickens. Postmaster General Montgomery Blair disagreed.

He favored sending supplies and reinforcements to Sumter and introduced Lincoln to someone with a plan for how to do so, a former naval officer and steamship captain named Gustavus Vasa Fox, who was married to the sister of Blair's wife. Fox's plan was to bring supplies and 200 reinforcements on a merchant ship, transfer them to New York ferryboats, and then slip them into Fort Sumter in the middle of the night. As most of the fleet was overseas or in ordinary (out of service), there were only a few naval vessels available. Welles did agree to provide the converted merchant ship *Pocahontas*, the new screw sloop *Pawnee*, the old but powerful sidewheel frigate *Powhatan*, and the revenue cutter *Harriet Lane*.

The plan was approved by Lincoln, but it proved unsuccessful, largely due to factors outside Fox's control. When Fox arrived off Charleston Harbor aboard the merchant ship early on the morning of 12 April 1861, he found only the *Harriet Lane*. The *Powhatan* had been diverted to Pensacola without Welles's knowledge, and the others had been scattered by a storm. While Fox awaited the other ships, the Confederates began shelling Fort Sumter. Lincoln had warned the governor of South Carolina that an attempt would be made to resupply the fort, leaving him the onus of starting hostilities and hence outraging Northern public opinion. Fearing a huge body of federal troops would be sent to Fort Sumter, the governor and Jefferson Davis elected to open hostilities. The fort surrendered before Fox could enter the harbor.[5]

Far from blaming Fox, Lincoln was impressed by his energy, courage, and imagination. He appointed Fox as Welles's chief clerk and then, with congressional approval, assistant secretary of the navy. Welles and Fox would become partners in running the navy and serve together through the end of the war.

Immediately upon learning of the attack on Fort Sumter, Lincoln called for 75,000 volunteers to serve in the army for ninety days. Davis quickly retaliated. Possessing only a dozen tiny warships contributed by various Southern states,[6] he could take little action against the Union navy, but on 17 April he invited private citizens to fit out privateers to cruise against Northern shipping. This proposal had only a brief success. Lincoln immediately declared a blockade of every Southern port, and soon the privateers had no place to send their prizes.[7] Until Union warships were available to implement the blockade, however, the Confederacy had the opportunity of sending cotton to Europe, where it could be sold and the proceeds used to buy weapons; instead, it put an unofficial but nevertheless effective embargo on cotton in the hope of pressuring Britain and France, whose textile mills were dependent on American cotton, into recognizing the Confederacy.

This proved a serious mistake. Britain and France had a year's worth of cotton on hand, much of the British public was against slavery, and French emperor Napoleon III was unwilling to act without British support.[8] The blockade was of dubious legality, but the British, who expected to make use of blockades in the future, were more than willing to bend the rules so as not to challenge it. To avoid involvement in the war, they recognized the Confederates as belligerents, which provided some justification for the United States blockading a country whose existence it didn't recognize. British neutrality was put in peril the following November, however, when a Union warship seized the Confederate diplomats James Mason and John Slidell en route to Britain and France. Wisely the U.S. government backed down and released them.[9] The immediate danger of war with Britain and its mighty navy quickly passed. The Confederates eventually abandoned the embargo, but it was too late. Between the increasingly effective Union blockade and the need to plant crops to feed the Confederate army, cotton exports declined to a fraction of prewar totals. This had devastating effects on the Confederate economy. Ironically, one of the main markets for Southern cotton (and source of specie for the Confederacy) was the Union states, which used corrupt speculators and even members of the Union armed forces to purchase it for resale to Northern factories and foreign customers.

The Union established its blockade with surprising speed, even though it was far from being totally effective. This was largely due to the newly established Blockade Strategy Board, composed of one of the most promising captains in the navy, two scientists, and a leading army engineer. It quickly drafted plans for implementing the blockade. This was the first of numerous boards to advise the president, a sharp contrast to the amateur nature of Confederate administration.

Meanwhile, Welles and Fox purchased almost 100 merchant ships and converted them into warships. They also quickly built 23 screw gunboats that were ideal for shallow Southern waters.[10] In November the Union navy captured Port Royal Sound, a large anchorage between Savannah and Charleston. The Union fleet of 17 warships demolished two Confederate forts guarding the sound. The 13,000 troops that accompanied the fleet were not needed except for occupying the forts, which surrendered to the navy. The capture of Port Royal Sound permitted the navy to provide coal, other supplies, and services to the blockading squadron without its having to return to Northern ports. The navy, with army assistance, also seized Hatteras Inlet, giving access to Pamlico Sound,

North Carolina. Early in 1862 it helped capture Roanoke Island, North Carolina, and helped force the surrender of Fort Pulaski at the entrance to the Savannah River.[11]

III

The rapid buildup and quick use of the Union navy posed a great challenge to Secretary of the Confederate Navy Stephen Mallory, a former chairman of the U.S. Senate Committee for Naval Affairs.[12] Mallory was knowledgeable, energetic, and personable, but prone to wishful thinking and neither a forceful nor an inspiring leader. Moreover, there was little initially he could do. Private investors were more interested in acquiring vessels to run supplies into Southern ports (called blockade runners) than in fitting out privateers. He tried building steam-powered gunboats to protect Southern ports, but this strained Southern capabilities (particularly in supplying engines), and they were as ineffective as Jefferson's gunboats had been. Somewhat more successful was the Confederate navy's sending warships to prey on Union shipping in order to siphon Union warships away from the blockade. The first such ship, the *Sumter*, captured eighteen prizes before being trapped at Gibraltar by Union ships and then abandoned. A dozen more such cruisers eventually were used, the most successful being the British-built *Alabama, Florida,* and *Shenandoah.* The British government gradually tightened its precautions against the Confederacy, taking possession of ships built in British dockyards under false pretenses for conversion into warships and hence undermining British neutrality. The French government subsequently followed suit, foiling Confederate plans to purchase abroad oceangoing ironclads to break the Union blockade. (The Confederates did repurchase a French-built ironclad from the Danish navy at the beginning of 1865, but it was too late to reach the South before the end of the war.) The cruisers harmed the reputation of the Confederacy abroad, and although they captured more than 200 ships and ruined many shipowners unable to meet increased insurance costs, they did not draw off enough Union warships to affect the blockade significantly.[13]

During his career in the Senate, Mallory had advocated building modern ships like the Stevens battery and was well aware of European naval developments. His solution for the Confederate navy was to construct a warship clad in iron that could not only drive the Union navy away from Southern ports but could even carry the war to Northern ports. His problem was the shortage of ships and engines in Southern ports. Luckily for him, there was a ship that he could use. Lincoln's response to Fort Sumter, the establishment of a blockade and the call for 75,000 volunteers, caused four more states, Virginia, Arkansas, North Carolina, and Tennessee, to secede. Across the Elizabeth River from Norfolk was the great naval base at Gosport with more than 1,000 cannon, 300,000 pounds of gunpowder, and an enormous quantity of naval stores, a prize as valuable as the weapons of Ticonderoga had been to the Continental army in 1775. There also were a dozen warships. Most of them, like the giant ship of the line *Pennsylvania*, were obsolete, but also present was the nearly new steam frigate *Merrimack*, out of service because of its unreliable engines. When Virginia seceded, a mob appeared at the gates of the navy yard. The commander, fearing the responsibility of causing bloodshed, panicked and scuttled (deliberately sank) several ships. When the *Pawnee* arrived with reinforcements, its captain also panicked. He ordered the shipyard burned, and then departed.

The job was incomplete (like the British burning of the great French naval base of Toulon in 1793). The cannon and other supplies and facilities escaped destruction as did the hull of the *Merrimack*, which had been partly underwater when the dockyard was burned. Mallory decided to raise the hull, remove the ruined superstructure, and convert the ship into a warship clad in iron. He renamed it the *Virginia*.[14]

The *Virginia* was not the first ironclad to be completed. The first were far smaller. They were converted into Union warships along the Ohio and Mississippi Rivers. Although they had little impact on the subsequent history of the warship, they had an enormous impact on the Civil War.

IV

Just as they had been during the War of 1812, the inland naval battles during the Civil War were as important as those at sea. When the war began, Lincoln's first army general-in-chief, Winfield Scott, proposed a strategy for winning the war with a minimum of bloodshed. His so-called Anaconda plan involved using the Union navy to strangle the Confederacy by blockading the Confederate coast while Union gunboats and troops descended the Mississippi to cut the Confederacy in two. The gunboats accompanying the troops down the Mississippi were to be under army control, but Welles sent a very capable naval officer, Commander John Rodgers, to supervise their construction. Rodgers first selected three sidewheel riverboats to convert into warships by covering their superstructures with thick oak planks to protect them against small arms fire from the shore. These "timberclads," the *Conestoga*, the *Lexington*, and the *Tyler*, did as much to win the war as any Union warships, but they were quickly followed by stronger

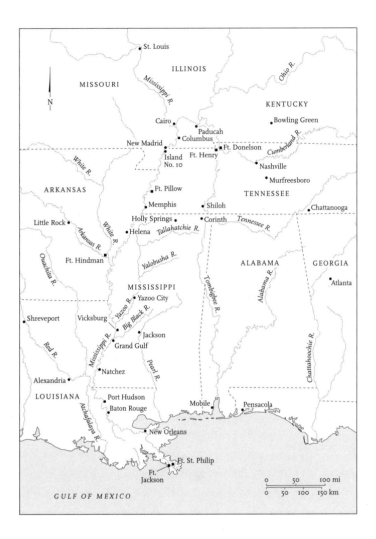

The Mississippi Valley

vessels. James Eads, a St. Louis engineer and businessman, was given a contract to build seven ships propelled by a central paddlewheel. Their gun decks were protected by a wood and iron casemate (a structure with a roof and slanting sides built atop the deck). These ships, the *Cairo, Carondelet, Cincinnati, Louisville, Mound City, Pittsburg,* and *St. Louis,* were launched in October 1861, a mere three months after construction began, and entered service in January 1862. They were commonly called "Pook turtles" or "Pook's turtles" because naval constructor Samuel Pook helped design them and because of their odd appearance. Meanwhile two other riverboats were converted into ironclads, the *Benton* and *Essex.* Command of the dozen ships of the army's Western Flotilla was given to a veteran naval officer, Captain Andrew Foote, although he was required to operate under army supervision.

The Confederacy could not match the Union effort. Although it had a number of wooden gunboats, some of them equipped like Confederate ironclads with a ram at their front to puncture the hulls of Union ships, it never had more than one ironclad operational at the same time on the Mississippi or on the tributaries of the Mississippi and Ohio Rivers. Moreover, Commodore George Hollins, the Confederate naval commander on the upper Mississippi, was second rate.[15]

The first accomplishment of the Western Flotilla was in November 1861. The *Lexington* and *Tyler* gave support to a 3,000-man detachment of troops commanded by Brigadier General U. S. Grant that landed near Belmont, Missouri, just across the Mississippi River from the heavily fortified Confederate base of Columbus, Kentucky. The timberclads covered the return of the troops to their transports when Confederate reinforcements arrived.[16] The following month the

Conestoga, which had been patrolling the Tennessee and Cumberland Rivers near their junction with the Ohio, reported that the Confederates were constructing ironclad ships on the two rivers upstream (south) of the Confederate forts being constructed near the Kentucky-Tennessee border. These forts, Fort Henry on the east bank of the Tennessee River and Fort Donelson on the west bank of the Cumberland River, were the center of Confederate General Albert S. Johnston's western defense line that extended from Columbus to the rail center of Bowling Green in central Kentucky. The two forts were far from equal, however. Fort Donelson, situated like Columbus on a bluff well above water level, was very formidable, while the smaller Fort Henry, built near river level, was vulnerable to ironclads. Johnston's defense line was like a house whose back and side doors were locked and bolted, but whose front entrance was only a screen door. Belatedly the Confederates began to construct a stronger fort on the opposite bank of the Tennessee River, but because the Union river ironclads were completed so quickly, they didn't have time to finish it.

Major General Henry Halleck, commanding the Union troops in the region of the Mississippi River, ordered Grant and Foote to attack Fort Henry as soon as the new ironclads were ready. On 6 February 1862 the *Carondelet, Cincinnati, Essex, St. Louis, Lexington, Tyler,* and *Conestoga* attacked. The fort, built at water level, was indefensible because the Tennessee River was in flood. It surrendered after a brief bombardment by the Western Flotilla, although the 3,000-man garrison escaped. The first of Grant's 18,000 troops arrived thereafter to accept the formal surrender. The *Conestoga, Tyler,* and *Lexington* immediately continued upriver, the first two going as far as Florence, Alabama. They captured the incomplete ironclad

Eastport and destroyed a vital bridge over the Tennessee, thereby breaking the rail links between the various parts of the Columbus to Bowling Green defense line. Johnston decided to retreat to a defense line extending from Memphis on the Mississippi River to Nashville.[17]

To protect his retreat Johnston ordered the recently reinforced 18,000- or 20,000-man garrison at Fort Donelson to hold out as long as possible. Foote and Grant, however, moved quickly. Fort Donelson was located on a bluff above the Cumberland, a dozen miles east of Fort Henry. Thus it was able to repulse a 14 February attack by the *St. Louis, Louisville, Pittsburg, Carondelet, Conestoga,* and *Tyler,* when gunfire could not reach it. The inept Confederate commanders, however, let their garrison be trapped by Grant's army. They fled, leaving a subordinate to surrender the fort and most of the troops. The *Carondelet* and *Cairo* then sailed up the Cumberland River almost as far as Nashville. Soon thereafter Grant sent a detachment upriver on transports to occupy Nashville, which Johnston had abandoned. Grant's troops were joined by Union troops advancing from Bowling Green. The loss of Nashville, one of the largest cities of the South as well as a major manufacturing center, was a serious blow to the Confederacy.[18]

Johnston continued his retreat until his army reached the rail center of Corinth, Mississippi, where it was reinforced by troops from New Orleans, Mobile, and Columbus, Kentucky. When the Confederates evacuated Columbus, they left a 5,000-man garrison downriver at Island Number Ten in the Mississippi (just south of the Kentucky-Tennessee border) and the adjacent shoreline. The island, just off the west bank, was protected by its own guns as well as those on the east bank. Although he had been seriously wounded during the attack on

Fort Donelson, Foote remained in command of the Western Flotilla, which provided the new *Benton* and the veteran *Cincinnati, St. Louis, Mound City, Louisville, Pittsburg, Carondelet,* and *Conestoga* in support of a Union army on the west bank. Their bombardment, however, could not silence the enemy guns. Finally the *Carondelet* and *Pittsburg* steamed past the enemy guns, permitting Union troops to cross the Mississippi and trap the Confederates. They surrendered on the night of 7–8 April. Meanwhile the *Lexington* and *Tyler* were helping repulse a massive Confederate attack on Grant's army at Pittsburg Landing on the Tennessee. During the first day of the battle, named the Battle of Shiloh after a nearby church, Johnston was killed. That night the Union timberclads protected the movement of reinforcements across the river, permitting Grant to counterattack. The defeated Confederates retreated to Corinth, which was captured after a lengthy siege.[19]

v

The Confederate concentration of troops to fight the Battle of Shiloh left New Orleans, the South's largest city, virtually without soldiers. It depended for its protection on its downstream river defenses, Fort Jackson and Fort St. Philip, and a river fleet consisting chiefly of the small ironclad *Manassas* and two large ironclads, the *Mississippi* and *Louisiana*, still under construction. Commander David Dixon Porter of the Union navy, the son of the captain of the *Essex* during its celebrated cruise in the Pacific in 1812–14, approached Fox and Welles with a plan to reduce the Confederate forts. He proposed to use mortars mounted on small schooners to direct vertical fire on the forts, a weapon that had been effective during the Crimean War. (Porter had visited one of the French mortar ships used in the war.) Fox and Welles not only agreed but appointed Porter to construct and command these bomb vessels. They would need a fleet to accompany them. To its command Fox and Welles appointed David Glasgow Farragut, former captain of the *Brooklyn*, a Southerner who had come north when Virginia left the Union. By honoring his oath to the United States at great personal cost, he, like the great Virginia-born soldier George Thomas, showed extraordinary moral courage. The choice of Farragut, who was not high on the seniority list, proved inspired. With his meticulous preparation for combat, his rapport with his captains, and his extraordinary courage, Farragut came to resemble Horatio Nelson. He and Porter had a family connection, as Porter's parents had taken in the young Farragut after the death of his mother; moreover, Farragut had sailed as a midshipman aboard the *Essex* with Porter's father.[20]

Welles named Farragut as commander of the West Gulf Blockading Squadron, one of the four components of the Union blockade of Southern ports. (The others were the North Atlantic, South Atlantic, and East Gulf Blockading Squadrons).[21] At the beginning of April 1862, his squadron entered the Mississippi and approached the Confederate forts, arriving before the defenders could finish work on the ironclads *Mississippi* and *Louisiana*. It was accompanied by transports carrying 7,000 troops. Disappointingly, Porter's twenty-one bomb vessels failed to silence the Confederate guns. On the night of 23–24 April Farragut ran past the forts with six screw sloops (*Hartford, Pensacola, Oneida, Brooklyn, Richmond*, and *Iroquois*), six newly built screw gunboats (*Cayuga, Katahdin, Kineo, Wissahickon, Sciota*, and *Pinola*), the sidewheel frigate *Mississippi*, the sailing sloop *Portsmouth*, and the converted merchant ship *Varuna*. Three other ships, the gunboats *Kennebec*, *Itasca*, and *Winona*, arriving after daybreak, were forced to turn back. The *Varuna* was sunk by two Confederate gunboats north of the forts. The Confederate ironclad *Louisiana* participated in the battle but, unable to move on its own power, it was used only as a floating battery. The Confederates would have had more gunboats had Mallory not withheld them in the belief that any Union attack would come downriver from the north.[22] On 25 April Farragut's fleet reached New Orleans and began negotiations for taking possession of it. Meanwhile the downstream forts surrendered to Porter; the small Confederate ironclad *Manassas* and the incomplete ironclads *Mississippi* and *Louisiana* were destroyed by their crews. Thereafter Union troops occupied the forts and the city of New Orleans.

Although he would rather have attacked the port of Mobile next, Farragut followed orders to remain on the Mississippi. On the night of 27–28 June, the *Hartford*, *Oneida*, *Brooklyn*, *Richmond*, *Iroquois*, *Wissahickon*, *Sciota*, *Kennebec*, *Ketahdin*, *Pinola*, and *Winona* attempted to steam past Confederate gun batteries atop the 200-foot bluffs of Vicksburg. Although the *Brooklyn*, *Kennebec*, and *Ketahdin* were forced to turn back, the other ships made it. On 1 July Farragut was joined by the Western Flotilla ironclads *Benton*, *Carondelet*, *Cincinnati*, and *Louisville* north of the Confederate defenses. The Western Flotilla was now commanded by Flag Officer Charles Davis. He replaced Foote, who reluctantly had taken medical leave. Davis already had captured the important river city of Memphis after fighting off a squadron of Confederate gunboats. Unfortunately Davis had no troops with him, Farragut had brought too few to capture Vicksburg, and General Halleck, who had recently captured Corinth, refused to spare any of his. Vicksburg thus escaped, giving the Confederates the opportunity to send it reinforcements and to extend the fortifications along the bluffs of the Yazoo River that flowed into the Mississippi several miles upriver from the city.[23] In spite of their failure to capture Vicksburg, the Union army and navy in less than six months had captured New Orleans, Nashville, and Memphis, three of the South's most important cities. They had attacked before Confederate defenses on land and water were ready; their leaders Grant, Farragut, Foote, and Porter were among the greatest in American military and naval history. Confederate defense preparations were tardy, its military commanders were inept, and its naval forces were ineffective. Perhaps most importantly, Union naval mobilization had been enormously superior to Confederate mobilization.

VI

Farragut soon had to run the batteries in the opposite direction lest his squadron be trapped by the falling water level of the Mississippi. As he prepared to depart, the Confederate ironclad *Arkansas* emerged from the Yazoo River and passed successfully through Davis and Farragut's surprised fleets. With Farragut's return to New Orleans, the *Arkansas* posed a threat to the downriver Union garrisons. Near Baton Rouge, however, it ran aground and was set afire by its crew when the river ironclad *Essex* (which had accompanied Farragut) appeared. An attack on Baton Rouge by 3,000 Confederates was repulsed, but Confederates soon fortified nearby Port Hudson.

In spite of the check, Farragut was named the navy's first rear admiral. The Western Flotilla was transferred to the navy and renamed the Mississippi squadron; Porter was appointed its commander. At year's end a Union army commanded by

William T. Sherman attacked the Yazoo portion of the Vicksburg defenses, but failed. Union gunboats were unable to bombard the Confederate defenses on the bluffs high above the river. The stalemate continued with the Mississippi squadron controlling the Mississippi above Vicksburg, while the Confederates controlled the river between Vicksburg and Port Hudson. In January 1863, however, a joint attack by the Union army and navy captured Fort Hindman on the Arkansas River (with nearly 5,000 prisoners) thanks largely to the ironclads *Louisville, Cincinnati*, and *Baron de Kalb* (formerly *St. Louis*) and timberclad *Lexington*.

There was a similar stalemate in Tennessee where, after an unsuccessful Confederate incursion into Kentucky, the two sides faced each other near Nashville. Although hindered in accumulating supplies by low water on the Cumberland River, the Union army was able to advance south from the city in December. It captured Murfreesboro, thirty-five miles from Nashville, after a fierce battle at Stones River. Although it could advance no further, rising water on the Cumberland permitted resupply of the army.[24] In Virginia, too, 1862 ended in stalemate after a bloody campaign in which naval power had played a significant part.

VII

While the Western Flotilla's timberclads and ironclads were winning their first great victories, the Confederate navy yard at Gosport was desperately trying to complete the conversion of the *Virginia*. Although it had a casemate of wood and iron like the "Pook turtles," it was almost 100 feet longer than the Union ironclads and drew 22 feet of water compared with their 6 feet draft. There were no engines in the South large enough to replace the *Merrimack*'s balky ones, and attempts to import engines from abroad were halfhearted and ineffectual; the old ones had to do. The Tredegar Iron Works at Richmond had to adjust its machinery to produce armor plate thick enough for the *Virginia*'s casemate and then had difficulty in transporting the armor to Norfolk by rail. Thus it took more than half a year to convert the *Virginia*, which was not commissioned until 17 February 1862.[25]

Meanwhile, on 3 August 1861 Congress appropriated funds to build its own ironclads for harbor and coastal defense. It then appointed a board to consider proposals on how to do so. The board considered seventeen proposals and approved three of them. One of the ironclads constructed was the *Galena*, whose armor proved insufficient. Another was the huge but slow *New Ironsides*, which greatly resembled the French broadside ironclad *Gloire*. It was and remained the only American warship capable of fighting European ironclads at sea, but it was of limited use against the Confederacy because it drew too much water; moreover, it was not completed until August 1862. The third was designed by the brilliant John Ericsson, who had designed the revolutionary *Princeton* twenty years earlier. His ironclad wooden ship, the *Monitor*, drew only 10.3 feet of water and its deck was barely above the waterline.[26] Barely as large as a "Pook turtle," it had a crew of only 50, compared to the *Virginia*'s 300. Because of its appearance it was compared to a cheese box on a raft or a tin can on a shingle, but it was as strong as the *Virginia* and much more maneuverable. Its massive rotating turret enclosed two 11-inch guns (i.e., guns that fired a shell 11 inches in diameter, the same size as the guns of the *Graf Spee* of 1939). Some of its successors had 15-inch guns, the same size as those of the *Bismarck* and *Tirpitz.* Turrets like those of the *Monitor* would house the principal armament of battleships for the next century.[27] The *Virginia* carried 10 guns along the sides, back, and front of its casemate, but none fired more than a 9-inch shell.

Perhaps most important and most amazing about Ericsson's ship is how quickly it was built. Begun on 25 October 1861, it was launched on 30 January 1862 and commissioned on 25 February, a delivery time comparable to that of Eads's far less complicated and innovative ironclads.

On 8 March 1862 the *Virginia* left Gosport and entered Hampton Roads, near the mouth of Chesapeake Bay. Between 1 and 5 p.m., it sank the sailing frigate *Congress* and sailing sloop *Cumberland* and forced the steam frigate *Minnesota* aground. Franklin Buchanan, the flag officer aboard the *Virginia*, was wounded. (As it had no captain aboard, it was commanded the next day by its executive officer, Catesby ap Roger Jones.) When it hoisted anchor the next day to finish off the *Minnesota*, it encountered the *Monitor,* which had arrived from New York the previous evening. The two ironclads fought all morning, until the *Virginia* returned to port. Neither vessel was seriously damaged, but the battle was a strategic victory for the Union, because it preserved access to Fort Monroe on the north shore of Hampton Roads for a large Union army that arrived at the end of the month.[28] Neither the *Virginia,* needed by the South for protection of the Norfolk area and the James River, nor the *Monitor,* needed by the Union to protect Hampton Roads and the York River, was willing to risk another battle. During April the Union army, commanded by Major General George McClellan, advanced along the York River toward Richmond, although its advance was delayed by the need to besiege Yorktown. Once Yorktown was captured, Confederate forces at Norfolk were so isolated that they abandoned the city and on 11 May destroyed the *Virginia*.[29]

The *Monitor's* success in combat led Welles and Fox to construct many more ships like it. By May 1865, forty-one monitors (and seven shallow draft river monitors) had been launched and another ten were under construction, the monitors growing larger as the war progressed. In comparison, the South began some thirty casemate ironclads like the *Virginia*, of which some twenty were completed, but none of them was as heavy as the *Virginia*. This hardly is surprising, as by mid-1862 the South's best shipbuilding facilities—at Gosport, New Orleans, and Memphis—were in Union hands.

Ultimately the monitor as a type was only a limited success. Although after the war the monitor *Monadnock* rounded Cape Horn and the monitor *Miantonomoh* crossed the Atlantic, they had too little freeboard (distance between the deck and waterline) to be safe beyond coastal waters; the *Monitor* itself sank in a storm off Cape Hatteras at the end of 1862. They were slow, as was the rate of fire of their guns. Gradually they were replaced by larger, safer, more powerful ships; during the early part of World War II the British built the last two warships called monitors (used for coastal bombardment).[30]

After the destruction of the *Virginia*, the Union navy had the chance to steam up the James River to Richmond, destroy the Tredegar Iron Works, foundries, and shipyards along its waterfront, and possibly even force the surrender of the Confederate capital. As a squadron including the *Monitor, Galena*, and experimental ironclad *Naugatuck* disposed of obstacles in the river, the Confederates, including the former crew of the *Virginia*, rushed work on fortifications at Drewry's Bluff, only eight miles downstream of the city. They finished just in time to repulse the Union squadron, which was hampered by the ironclads' limited ability to elevate their guns.

General McClellan, now to the east of the city, weighed the possibility of shifting his army to the James, where he would have naval support for his final attack. He delayed, however, to take advantage of the opportunity. Then the choice was taken out of his hands. Heavily reinforced by the army of Thomas "Stonewall" Jackson, the Confederates under their new commander, Robert E. Lee, attacked McClellan's northern flank. During the Seven Days' Battle of 26 June to 1 July, they forced him away from his York River base to the James. During the last day's battle at Malvern Hill, near the James River, McClellan had the support of the *Galena* and two Union gunboats (although their fire was not very effective). Unfortunately McClellan's success in reaching the James did not lead to a new advance on Richmond. Shaken by the ferocity of the Confederate attack, he refused to advance without a large number of reinforcements that Lincoln was unwilling to provide. McClellan eventually was ordered to return to Fort Monroe. Two years later the Union army would suffer 55,000 casualties in order to reach the James.[31]

Before all of McClellan's army could be shifted to the new front between Washington and Richmond, Lee won the second Battle of Bull Run. Unwilling to attack heavily fortified Washington (whose defenses were strengthened by Union control of the Potomac River), he invaded Maryland well upstream of where the river was navigable. Defeated at the Battle of Antietam, he retreated to central Virginia, where the campaign ended with the repulse of a Union attack at Fredericksburg. Although the Union captured little territory during the second half of 1862, it did repulse Confederate invasions of

Kentucky and Maryland. The victory at Antietam gave Lincoln the opportunity to issue his Emancipation Proclamation, transforming the nature of the war. Moreover, by year's end the danger had receded that the Confederacy would be recognized by Britain or France (a threat that had been caused by high unemployment among British and French textile workers as a result of the cotton shortage). This was less a result of the Emancipation Proclamation, which initially was poorly received abroad, than it was of Union military victories, favorable results for the Republican Party in midterm elections, and the danger of a war with the United States that could not only menace Canada but also match the British navy in American coastal waters if not at sea.[32] The South was far from defeated, but it had lost its best chance to win the war.

VIII

The new year began with an embarrassing defeat for the Union. On 1 January 1863 Confederate gunboats and troops surprised a Union garrison and small squadron at Galveston, Texas, and recaptured the port. Texas, however, remained a backwater. In spite of the stalemates in Mississippi, Tennessee, and Virginia, Welles and Fox were obsessed with capturing Charleston, where the war had begun. Lincoln, wishing a victory before the opening of the summer campaigning season, agreed to their plans. When Union army attempts to reach Charleston Harbor failed, the navy tried to bombard Fort Sumter into surrender, as had been successful at Fort Henry, Fort Pulaski off Savannah, and the forts at Port Royal Sound. It was hoped that this would enable the Union fleet to reach Charleston. The attempt was made on 7 April 1763 by a fleet that included the *New Ironsides* and seven monitors, but it failed. Confederate defenses were too strong, and the monitors' rate of fire was too slow.[33] The navy would have to make its major contribution during 1863 by supporting the army and by applying indirect pressure on the Confederacy.

In spite of its failure to capture Vicksburg or Charleston, the navy still controlled not only the upper portion of the Mississippi but also major portions of the eastern seaboard, including the North Carolina sounds south of Richmond. During the winter of 1862–63, General Lee detached 18,000 troops under Lieutenant General James Longstreet in an unsuccessful attempt to clear the southern approaches to Richmond. These troops had not yet returned to Lee's Army of Northern Virginia when the Army of the Potomac attacked Southern positions near Chancellorsville in early May. Lee's army narrowly escaped a disastrous defeat. When it mounted its own offensive into Pennsylvania the following month, four of its best brigades, nearly 10,000 men, were retained in North Carolina (while two inferior brigades were substituted for them). Lee had hoped not only for them but also for troops from Charleston, but he obtained neither.[34] The navy thus played an indirect part in the closely fought 1–3 July Union victory at Gettysburg.

Its role was much more direct in a great victory that occurred the following day, the surrender of Vicksburg.[35] The capture of Vicksburg was the culmination of a campaign that began in March when Farragut's *Hartford* steamed upstream past the defenses of Port Hudson, regaining control of the Mississippi below Vicksburg. On the night of 16–17 April, the ironclads *Benton, Louisville, Carondelet, Mound City, Pittsburg,* and *Lafayette* of Porter's Mississippi squadron slipped downstream past Vicksburg. A week later Porter was joined south of the city by five transports carrying rations and forage. Having failed to find any other way to attack Vicksburg, General Grant marched 23,000 troops down the west bank of the Mississippi and on 30 April used the transports to ferry them across the river. After landing more than fifty river miles south of Vicksburg, Grant then conducted the war's closest equivalent to Napoleon's classic *manoeuvre sur les derrières*,[36] winning several battles, dispersing the only army that could move to the city's relief, and then driving the defenders of Vicksburg into their own lines and besieging them. Ironclads from the Mississippi squadron played a large part in the campaign. Just before Grant crossed the Mississippi, some of the ships that Porter left behind when he slipped past Vicksburg (including the ironclads *Choctaw* and *Baron de Kalb* and timberclad *Tyler*) made a diversion by a simulated attack on the fortifications along the Yazoo. This fooled the Confederates into thinking the real danger to Vicksburg was from its north. Once the siege began, Porter's squadron played a vital part in the relentless bombardment that finally led to the surrender of the entire garrison of the key fortress on 4 July 1863. A Confederate attack on the river port of Helena, Arkansas, was defeated on the same day with the help of the timberclad *Tyler*. Five days later a Union army supported by Admiral Farragut accepted the surrender of Port Hudson. The Mississippi was now completely in Union hands. Later that month Union gunboats on the Ohio River played a vital part in trapping an entire Confederate raiding party that had dared to sneak across the river into southern Indiana before crossing into southern Ohio.[37]

During the summer a combined campaign of the Union army and navy was directed against the defenses of Charleston Harbor. Although they failed to breech the harbor's inner defenses, the army, assisted particularly by the mighty *New*

Ironsides, managed at the beginning of September to capture Fort Wagner, which protected the southern approach to the harbor. This substantially reduced the role of Charleston as a center of blockade running from Bermuda and the Bahamas.[38]

Meanwhile the Union army in Tennessee managed to capture Chattanooga without a fight. The Army of Tennessee, reinforced by two divisions from Lee's army, counterattacked. On 19–20 September it won the Battle of Chickamauga, drove the Union army back into Chattanooga, and then besieged it. The Union army was able to make use of the Tennessee River to break the siege of Chattanooga. It seized a position downstream of the city so it could send supplies via steamboat and then by a short journey overland. This replaced a demanding route by land over difficult terrain. Eventually the reinforced Union garrison captured the enemy positions overlooking the city and drove the besiegers back into northern Georgia.[39]

IX

The great Union victories of 1863 severely weakened the Confederacy. Grant, now commander in chief of the Union army, ordered simultaneous attacks on all fronts during 1864. The Mississippi squadron was deeply involved in the least successful of these attacks, the movement up the Red River toward Shreveport, Louisiana, supposedly to menace Texas, but in fact largely to obtain cotton for sale. When the Union army was beaten, units of the Mississippi squadron were trapped by the falling water level of the river. By constructing dams, the water level was raised enough that ten trapped ships escaped when the dam was breached.[40]

The two most important offensives were the Georgia campaign of General Sherman that led to the capture of Atlanta and the Virginia campaign directed by Grant himself that ended with his army besieging Richmond as well as the rail center of Petersburg to its south. The navy played little role in Sherman's campaign until he reached the sea at Savannah, but it greatly assisted Grant by covering the movement of reinforcements, such as the 16,000 men sent via Chesapeake Bay to the Pamunkey River at the end of May. It also maintained control of the James River, preventing three Richmond-built ironclads from moving downstream, and shielded the pontoon bridge used by Grant's army when it moved south of the Confederate capital to attack Petersburg in June (although for added protection a barrier of sunken ships also was constructed upstream). Control of the river was vital to the long siege of Richmond and Petersburg. Boundless supplies of food and war materiel passed along the river to Grant's massive supply depot at City Point, while the Confederate defenders went hungry. Desertion increased, making it difficult to man the defense lines as the Union siege lines were extended.

Lee's main hope of breaking the siege was a large detachment he had sent to invade the North. It crossed the Potomac upstream of its rapids and moved against the defenses of Washington. The North Atlantic Blockading Squadron sent an ironclad and several other ships to help defend the city. The Confederates retreated to the Shenandoah Valley of Virginia, where their army fought several battles and was virtually destroyed.[41]

The most important contribution of the navy to the 1864 campaign was Farragut's capture of the entrance to Mobile Bay, one of the chief blockade running ports of the Confederacy. Farragut's fleet included two monitors (*Tecumseh* and *Manhattan*), two river monitors (*Winnebago* and *Chickasaw*), nine screw sloops (*Hartford, Oneida, Brooklyn, Richmond, Monongahela,*

Lackawanna, Galena, Seminole, and *Ossipee*), one screw gunboat (*Kennebec*), and three sidewheel gunboats (*Metacomet,
Port Royal,* and *Octorara*). It had to brave the fire of the forts
guarding the entrance to the harbor and then to pass through
a minefield that sank the *Tecumseh.* (The mines, then called
"torpedoes," were the invention of the brilliant Confederate
scientist and naval officer Matthew Maury.) Finally it captured
a powerful ironclad, the *Tennessee,* the flagship of Admiral
Franklin Buchanan, as well as several gunboats.[42] Farragut's
victory, followed by the capture of Atlanta and the victories in
the Shenandoah Valley, restored confidence in Union victory
and helped President Lincoln win reelection.

The year ended with two more victories. On 15–16 December General George Thomas crushed the Confederate Army of
Tennessee at the Battle of Nashville. He was assisted by ships
from the Mississippi squadron commanded by a fellow Virginian, Acting Rear Admiral Samuel P. Lee, a distant cousin
of Robert E. Lee. Admiral Lee's flagship in the Cumberland
River was a Pook turtle, the *Cincinnati.* After the battle, however, the Mississippi squadron was unable to reach the pontoon bridge in the Tennessee River over which the remnants
of the Confederate army escaped.[43] Soon thereafter Sherman's
army, having marched across Georgia after capturing Atlanta, reached Savannah and established contact with the South
Atlantic Blockading Squadron. The Confederates evacuated
the city and retreated toward Charleston.

By the beginning of 1865 the Confederacy was on the verge
of defeat. Largely because of the blockade, Confederate currency was worthless, its railroad system was collapsing, and its
armies were starving. Sherman's army marched across South
Carolina, forcing the evacuation of Charleston. As it prepared

to enter North Carolina, the major obstacle it faced was the difficulty of obtaining supplies. In the most brilliant joint operation of the war, David Porter, now commanding the South Atlantic Blockading Squadron, helped capture Fort Fisher at the entrance to the Cape Fear River. This led to the capture of Wilmington, leaving faraway Galveston as the only open port in the Confederacy and opening a supply route for Sherman's army.[44] At the beginning of April, Lee's defense line at Petersburg was finally breached, forcing Lee to evacuate Richmond as well. His hopelessly outnumbered troops fled west, but could not escape the pursuing Union army. His surrender was followed by the surrender of the Confederate army in North Carolina and the eventual end of resistance. The last to surrender was the cruiser *Shenandoah*, which learned only on 2 August 1865 of the end of hostilities while far at sea.[45] The war that had begun with an unsuccessful naval relief effort ended with the surrender of the Confederacy's last warship.

The Union navy played a vital role in the war, both in the West where river gunboats proved indispensable to the success of the Union army and in the East where the blockade placed intolerable strains on Confederate logistics and communications. It could not have done so without overcoming the limitations that hitherto had held it back. Partly its success was based on the enormous growth of the American economy since 1815. The Lincoln administration, however, deserves credit for overcoming many harmful aspects of the colonial legacy. It created partnerships with industrialists like James Eads, raised unprecedented sums of money without crippling inflation, overcame opposition within the Northern states, expanded the scope of government, and balanced the needs of coast and interior. Its greatest naval failure was its inability to protect the shipping industry from Confederate raiders and foreign competition, but this did not seriously affect the Union war effort. Its legacy was of great benefit to the United States in general and the navy in particular. Indeed, the Civil War was the great turning point in American naval history.

X

From a Confederate perspective, the Civil War resembles the War of American Independence and the War of 1812, during which the overwhelming strength of the British navy eventually drove American warships from the sea. Like the American navy of those days, the Confederate navy was at an earlier stage of development than was its enemy. Not only was it hopelessly outnumbered, but its ships, unlike the fine frigates and sloops of the early American navy, were generally poorly built, leaky, and slow. Its most successful ships were the British-built commerce raiders *Florida*, *Alabama*, and *Shenandoah*. At its peak it had fewer than 5,000 crewmen for its ships, whereas the Union navy had more than 50,000. The Confederate army was grudging in transferring men to the navy, and unlike the Union navy, it did not enlist blacks or prisoners of war.[46] Its only two admirals, Raphael Semmes and Franklin Buchanan, did not command powerful fleets like those of Foote, Farragut, and Porter, but only small squadrons defending Richmond or Mobile. The tactics of Confederate squadrons were more individualistic than Union tactics. Whereas Union squadrons fought in formation, Confederate squadrons resorted to a disorganized melee like the battle off Memphis fought by the Confederate River Defense Fleet against the Western Flotilla. This was not just a matter of Southern individualism, like the rebel yell, but also a reflection of inexperience and technology. Lacking experience in operating in a line of battle, the Confederate navy made a virtue of necessity. The *Virginia* and other ironclads, as well as river gunboats, were equipped with rams, sharp reinforced attachments to their bows designed to puncture the hulls of wooden ships. The use of such weapons (which were much less popular with Union warships) dictated spontaneous attacks by individual ships.[47]

The Confederates also could not match the success of Union joint army-navy operations like the attack on Fort Fisher; their most prominent successes were the 1863 capture of Galveston and the 1864 capture of Plymouth, North Carolina, by Confederate troops aided by the ironclad *Albemarle*.[48]

Confederate naval failures were most often due to inadequate means. Even the Confederate naval bureaucracy was inadequate. Secretary of the Navy Mallory had no undersecretary like the experienced Fox to assist him, and his staff was tiny compared with the established bureaucracy of the Union navy. The Confederate navy suffered from shortages of armor plate, ship engines, and countless smaller items like reliable fuses for the shells fired by its ships. Thus it had great difficulty in building ships, and those it did complete were slow and unreliable.[49] Mallory himself was unrealistic, gambling on expensive weapons like the *Virginia* or the English-built "Laird rams" to produce a decisive victory just as Confederate armies gambled on winning the war by a decisive battle.

The backwardness of the Confederate navy was, of course, a reflection of the backwardness of the Confederacy itself. Economically, socially, culturally, and politically, the South was trapped in the past by the plantation system and the dominance of an authoritarian and selfish planter aristocracy.[50] Like the eighteenth-century American colonies and even the

Continental Congress, it attempted to fight a war by printing money (in this case treasury notes that served as currency) and issuing bonds. The results were almost 10,000 percent inflation and an army facing starvation. The Union, like the British during the Napoleonic Wars, raised unprecedented sums by a combination of taxation and borrowing. Although workers suffered as paper money depreciated to half the worth of specie, Northern farmers and businessmen prospered from the war, and Union troops and sailors were well fed. During a speech on 30 June 1862 Senator Samuel Pomeroy predicted that the United States would emerge strengthened from the war just as England had been strengthened by the war against Napoleon. He was prescient. Northern industrialization and self-sufficiency were stimulated by the war. Despite Southern efforts to achieve self-sufficiency, the Confederacy remained dependent on foreign imports and foreign markets. Access to them was gradually strangled as the tightening Union blockade greatly reduced the effectiveness of blockade running.[51]

The demands of the war forced the Confederate government to adopt measures such as the construction of railroads, the conscription of soldiers, the impressment of food, and even direct taxation, which were in contradiction to its philosophy of states' rights. (The Confederate Constitution even outlawed its central government undertaking internal improvements except for aids to navigation, a prohibition soon disregarded.) Its government, however, proved inadequate to the demands of modern warfare. Part of the problem was Jefferson Davis, who was indecisive, held grudges, let personal feelings affect his decisions, and equated loyalty to himself with loyalty to the Confederacy. Lincoln, Welles, and Secretary of War Edwin Stanton fired the unsuccessful and promoted those who could win, even if they had difficult characters like that of the demanding and ambitious David Dixon Porter. (The same toughness was shown by George Marshall of the army and Ernest King of the navy during World War II.) Davis continued to reward loyalty to the Southern cause even when his generals failed.[52] The problem, however, was more than just Davis. The Confederate government had difficulty in overcoming localism, such as that of state governors like Joseph Brown of Georgia and Zebulon Vance of North Carolina. They insisted that vital troops be used for protection of their states instead of being sent where they were most needed (such as the troops withheld from Lee before the Gettysburg campaign) and even hindered the raising of troops for the Confederate army. Moreover, major portions of the South, such as western Virginia and eastern Tennessee, were largely pro-Union. Worse still, despite all its efforts, the Confederacy could not raise the money it needed. The modernizing, centralizing, self-sufficient North was overcoming its colonial legacy of backwardness, and the Union navy reflected it. The Confederate navy did embrace technology. It developed casemate ironclads, mines, and even a moderately successful submarine,[53] while establishing facilities to construct ships, guns, and ammunition in places like Selma, Alabama, and Columbus, Georgia. Nevertheless it lacked the industrial base and financial resources to compete with the North. Its position was somewhat similar to France, which pioneered shell guns, screw warships, and ironclads but could not match Britain's industrial superiority.[54] Navies required an extremely high level of technological sophistication, organizational efficiency, and economic development. Because the South was so far behind the North, it could not counter the Union blockade. Its ironclads were not seagoing, and its cruisers were intended to capture merchant ships rather than warships. It lacked industrialists like Eads and Ericsson who, understanding mass production and subcontracting, could quickly build large numbers of strong, reliable warships.

Given the obstacles, the Confederate navy's building program was overly ambitious, like that of the Continental navy during the Revolution, draining scarce financial resources. After meeting the immediate needs of harbor and river defense, the Confederacy would have been better served by building or converting government-owned blockade runners rather than English-built commerce raiders and large casemate ironclads like the *Virginia*. They waited until near the end of the war to make the attempt.

The Confederate navy's worst failure, however, was its inability to counter the Union's inland navy. Without a major river navy, the Confederacy had to depend on land fortifications to defend itself from river ironclads and monitors. Where it could put gun batteries atop bluffs that naval gunfire could not reach (such as Drewry's Bluff, Columbus, Vicksburg, or even Fort Donelson), the Union navy could not be successful without the help of Northern troops. Forts at water level (such as those of Port Royal, New Orleans, and Fort Henry) were vulnerable; only at Charleston with its collection of forts with interlocking fire were Confederate defenders successful. Even mighty forts like Fort Wagner and Fort Fisher were vulnerable to joint army-navy assault because the Confederate navy provided little help for them. It was almost as unsuccessful at harbor defense as it was at river defense.

Nonetheless wars are not always won by the side with the most resources or the most modern economy, society, or government. Southerners expected to win the war just as their ancestors had won the War of American Independence. Like them they expected to defend their own territory against an invader facing great difficulties, particularly in terms of logistics and lines of communication. In other wars, too, the advantage of the defensive sometimes proved the decisive factor. A comparison of the Civil War and previous wars may help explain why the Confederacy failed.

XI

Was the destruction of the Confederacy inevitable, given the Union's far greater population and much higher level of industrial development? There certainly had been good reason for Confederate optimism, based on historical precedent. Admittedly there was one earlier case in North American history of an unsuccessful attempt at evading conquest: that of New France. A century before the Civil War, Great Britain had conquered New France despite enormous logistical difficulties and the great skill of Governor General the marquis de Vaudreuil and his commanders in the field like François-Gaston de Lévis.[55] New France, however, was not capable of growing or importing the food necessary to feed an army large enough to defend it. Moreover, it was outnumbered twenty to one in population by the neighboring British colonies and faced armies two to three times the size of its own. Nevertheless it required six campaigning years for the British to crush New France. The Confederacy faced far less daunting odds. A more immediate and encouraging historical precedent was the War of American Independence. The Confederates encountered many of the same problems as had their ancestors. Great Britain had a larger population and a much more developed economy than did the thirteen colonies. It had a navy to blockade the American coast and an excellent army with many well-trained generals. The Americans had to contend with British sympathizers in their midst, as well as with the various states' jealousy and suspicion. Runaway inflation nearly caused the collapse of the American economy and brought enormous hardship to the soldiers of the Continental army. In spite of a few talented amateur soldiers like Henry Knox and Nathanael Greene, most of Washington's subordinate generals were mediocre, and the Continental army often was bested in open combat. But the United States survived. Why didn't the Confederacy?

One major difference between the two wars was the success of American diplomacy and the failure of Confederacy diplomacy. What ultimately saved the United States was the financial and military assistance of its direct or indirect allies, France, Spain, and the Netherlands. The Confederates found no such assistance.

A second major difference was that the British, unlike the Union, had to mount a war largely from overseas.[56] They had to send supplies and reinforcements across the Atlantic Ocean, whereas Union armies had relatively short supply lines and at worst a river to cross to engage the enemy. Moreover with the invention of steam-powered locomotives and warships, it could use railroads and rivers to transport armies deep into the Confederacy. Finally, the Union had more ships for blockading than had the British, and Union bases were nearer than had been the British bases at Halifax, Britain, and the West Indies.

Because of the proximity of the enemy, the Confederacy's strategic problem most resembled those of Prussia during the Seven Years' War[57] or France during the French Revolution. Both of these countries were badly outnumbered by coalitions of enemies invading from virtually every direction. Both countries also were inferior at sea. The Prussians had virtually no navy whereas the navies of Sweden and Russia controlled the Baltic Sea to the north of Prussia. The French revolutionary navy was badly outnumbered and outclassed by the British navy. Yet both Prussia and revolutionary France survived. Why did not the Confederacy?

The Confederacy had several disadvantages that the Prussians and France did not. First, it was much less successful at making use of the advantage of interior lines. Although it sometimes managed to concentrate troops *within* a theater of war, such as at Shiloh or the Seven Days' Battle, on only one occasion, preceding the Battle of Chickamauga, did it shift a large number of troops between Virginia and the interior South. Because of the poor condition of Confederate railroads, moving troops was not easy,[58] and the Confederacy was vast in size compared with western and central Europe. The major problems in Confederate strategy, however, were the weakness and indecisiveness of Jefferson Davis's government and the localism it failed to overcome. Even Lee had difficulty thinking beyond Virginia, while at key moments localism and compartmentalization of command paralyzed Confederate strategy. Cavalry was retained in Mississippi in 1864, for example, rather than being used against Sherman's rail connections.[59] The absolutist ruler King Frederick II of Prussia had no resistance from local authorities with which to contend, and the French Committee of Public Safety crushed the cities and regions that attempted to resist it.

Second, the Union, like revolutionary France, developed a number of generals such as Grant, Sherman, Thomas, George Meade, and Philip Sheridan who could command large armies. Even Prussia had a second great army commander, Frederick the Great's brother Henry. The Confederate government, obsessed with seniority, only grudgingly rewarded talent. The only successful commander of a full-sized Confederate army was Lee, who refused to serve outside of the Virginia front, whereas Grant, like Frederick the Great, willingly went where he was most needed.

Third, Prussia and revolutionary France were able to finance their defense. Prussia received vital assistance from Britain and was able to extort money from conquered territory like the electorate of Saxony. The conquests of the French army were able to finance the French Revolution. The Confederacy, in contrast, was unable to feed its armies.

The Union navy played a part in starving the Confederacy. It was even more important because of its part in the joint army-navy operations that deprived the South of much of the coastal Carolinas and the forts and cities of the Mississippi, Tennessee, and Cumberland River valleys. The rivers of Prussia (except for the mouths of the Ems and Oder) and revolutionary France were impervious to naval power in the days before the steamship. Steam-powered ships were as revolutionary in warfare as was the railroad.

Finally, both Prussia and revolutionary France were opposed by coalitions of states that distrusted each other and cooperated only reluctantly. Eventually both opposing coalitions disintegrated.[60] In contrast the Confederacy faced a government more unified, more sophisticated, and more efficient than was its own, led by the strongest and most inspirational of American presidents. His government was able not only to mobilize the great resources of the Union but also to create a more powerful and modern United States, one that eventually would become the greatest military and naval power in the world.

SEVEN

Epilogue

During the Civil War the navy built or purchased some 600 ships, but once the war ended, most of them were demolished or sold; within half a dozen years only fifty or so were still in commission. The navy quickly reverted to its earlier limited function, that of protecting American trade. It was now reduced to a fraction of its former size.[1] Weary of war and taxes, the United States soon lost interest in maintaining its navy. Money for defense was spent mostly on the army, which received from the public most of the credit for winning the war and which still had the Indian nations of the interior West to subdue. The navy meanwhile not only had a small budget and rapidly deteriorating ships, but it also lost interest in technological invention, preferring to build wooden ships that could spend most of their time under sail, thereby saving money. Between 1872 and 1883 it launched two screw frigates and thirteen screw sloops (three with iron hulls that were classified as gunboats), but built nothing larger.[2] As late as 1881 a navy advisory board recommended that the navy continue to concentrate on building unarmored ships propelled by sail as well as steam.[3] In contrast, the British began building large turret ships without masts, the forerunners of the twentieth-century battleship.[4]

Although the mighty navy of Welles and Fox, Ericsson and Eads, Isherwood and Dahlgren, and Farragut and Porter was little more than a memory, still the underpinnings were present for the United States to become a great naval power. The United States was becoming one of the world's leading industrial powers, producing more steel by 1890 than any other country.[5] The federal government was no longer paralyzed by the debate over slavery, and states had lost power compared to it. With the completion of the transcontinental railroad and the subjugation of the Sioux and other great Indian nations, the West began losing its hold over the national imagination. The rise of colonialism abroad became a substitute to attract American expansionism, and foreign markets increasingly interested American business. During the 1880s, interest in the navy revived. In 1883 the navy began construction of its first modern cruisers, the *Atlanta*, *Boston*, and *Chicago*, and in 1888, its first battleship, the *Maine*.[6] By 1898 it was ready to fight its first European opponent since 1815, albeit a second-rate one, Spain. With a strong economy, an assertive government, a supportive public, and leaders and thinkers like Dewey, Mahan, Luce, Sampson, and Schley formed by the Civil War, the navy finally was ready to overcome the limitations imposed by its colonial legacy.[7]

The war with Spain also marked the beginning of a great reversal of American policy toward Europe. The eighty-year divorce of the United States from the European balance of power was coming to an end. Ahead lay America's entrance into World Wars I and II and the establishment of NATO. The colonial legacy would be turned on its head as America would attempt to lead Europe (sometimes successfully such as in the Bosnia crisis of the 1990s), instead of following Britain into wars that it did not consider its concern.

The United States, however, is still coming to grips with its colonial legacy as it debates America's place in the world, the role of the central government, and the applicability of European social, cultural, and political models. Some of the most admirable aspects of the American experiment, such as its tradition of self-government and its remarkable ethnic and religious diversity, began during the colonial period. There are other and more controversial survivals from the colonial past, however. Beliefs like isolationism and American exceptionalism as well as aspects of American culture like obsession with guns, distrust of government, and hatred of taxes have colonial origins. Even the navy, the world's largest and most modern, faces new challenges from nimble and elusive enemies. For it, as for the United States as a whole, the biggest challenge may be to overcome a sentimental attachment to past ways of doing things in order to embrace change as the path of progress.

Notes and Suggested Further Reading

ONE. THE AMERICAN COLONIES AND THE BRITISH NAVY

1. For the founding of the Spanish and French colonies, see Kenneth R. Andrews, *Trade, Plunder, and Settlement: Maritime Enterprise and the Genesis of the British Empire, 1480–1630* (Cambridge: Cambridge University Press, 1984); Hugh Thomas, *Rivers of Gold: The Rise of the Spanish Empire* (London: Weidenfeld and Nicolson, 2003); Henry Kamen, *Empire: How Spain Became a World Power, 1492–1763* (New York: HarperCollins, 2003); and David Hackett Fischer, *Champlain's Dream* (New York: Simon & Schuster, 2008). J. H. Elliot, *Empires of the Atlantic World: Britain and Spain in America, 1492–1830* (New Haven: Yale University Press, 2006) compares the British and Spanish colonies in the Western Hemisphere, while James Pritchard, *In Search of Empire: The French in the Americas, 1670–1730* (Cambridge: Cambridge University Press, 2004), discusses the French colonies in North America and the Caribbean.

2. Alan Tully, "The Political Development of the Colonies after the Glorious Revolution," in *The Blackwell Encyclopedia of the American Revolution*, ed. Jack P. Green and J. R. Pole (Cambridge MA: Blackwell, 1991), 28–38, gives a brief summary and bibliography. Surveys of American colonial history include Alan Taylor,

American Colonies (New York: Penguin, 2001); Richard Middleton, *Colonial America: A History, 1607–1760* (Cambridge MA: Blackwell, 1992); Walter A. McDougall, *Freedom Just Around the Corner: A New American History, 1585–1828* (New York: HarperCollins, 2004); Daniel K. Richter, *Before the Revolution: America's Ancient Pasts* (Cambridge: Belknap Press of Harvard University Press, 2011).

3. For an introduction to the administration of the British Empire, see Ian K. Steele, "Metropolitan Administration of the Colonies, 1696–1775," in *Blackwell Encyclopedia of the American Revolution*, ed. Greene and Pole, 9–16. Brendan Simms, *Three Victories and a Defeat: The Rise and Fall of the First British Empire* (New York: Basic Books, 2009) details the importance of European considerations.

4. For this convergence, see Jack P. Greene, *Understanding the American Revolution: Issues and Actors* (Charlottesville: University Press of Virginia, 1995), 143–49.

5. Donald G. Schomette and Robert D. Haslach, *Raid on America: The Dutch Naval Campaign of 1672–1674* (Columbia: University of South Carolina Press, 1988); Francis Jennings, *The Ambiguous Iroquois Empire: The Covenant Chain Confederation of Indian Tribes with English Colonies from Its Beginnings to the Lancaster Treaty of 1744* (New York: W. W. Norton, 1984), 122–30.

6. Emerson W. Baker and John G. Reid, *The New England Knight: Sir William Phips, 1651–1695* (Toronto: University of Toronto Press, 1998), 86–109; Gerald S. Graham, *Empire of the North Atlantic: The Maritime Struggle for North America*, 2nd ed. (Toronto: University of Toronto Press; London: Oxford University Press, 1958), 68–76; Douglas Edward Leach, *Arms for Empire: A Military History of the British Colonies in North America, 1607–1763* (New York: Macmillan; London: Collier-Macmillan, 1973), 92–99.

7. Leach, *Arms for Empire*, 144–54; Graham, *Empire of the North Atlantic*, 84–102. Graham also edited a collection of documents relating to the 1711 attack, *The Walker Expedition to Quebec, 1711* (London: Naval Records Society, 1953).

8. J. Leitch Wright Jr., *Anglo-Spanish Rivalry in North America* (Athens: University of Georgia Press, 1971), 61–69. For other Spanish colonies in what became the United States, see David J. Weber, *The Spanish Frontier in North America* (New Haven: Yale University Press, 1992).

9. Jonathan R. Dull, *The Age of the Ship of the Line: The British and French Navies, 1650–1815* (Lincoln: University of Nebraska Press, 2009), 37–40; Jon Parmenter and Mark Power Robison, "The Perils and Possibilities of Wartime Neutrality on the Edge of Empire: Iroquois and Acadians between the French and British in North America, 1744–1760," *Diplomatic History* 31 (2007): 167–206.

10. John Robert McNeill, *Atlantic Empires of France and Spain: Louisbourg and Havana, 1700–1763* (Chapel Hill: University of North Carolina Press, 1985).

11. Ralph David, *The Rise of the English Shipping Industry in the Seventeenth and Eighteenth Centuries* (London: Macmillan; New York: St. Martin's Press, 1962), 68; Neill R. Stout, *The Royal Navy in America, 1760–1775: A Study of Enforcement of British Colonial Policy in the Era of the American Revolution* (Annapolis: Naval Institute Press, 1973), 1–12; Jonathan R. Dull, *The French Navy and American Independence: A Study of Arms and Diplomacy, 1774–1787* (Princeton: Princeton University Press, 1975), 42–44; K. Jack Bauer, *A Maritime History of the United States: The Role of America's Seas and Waterways* (Columbia: University of South Carolina Press, 1988), 32–33; John J. McCusker and Russell R. Menard, *The Economy of British America, 1607–1789* (Chapel Hill: University of North Carolina Press, 1985), 318–21.

12. See Joseph J. Malone, *Pine Trees and Politics: The Naval Stores and Forest Policy in Colonial New England, 1691–1775* (Seattle: University of Washington Press, 1964); Robert Greenhaugh Albion, *Forests and Sea Power: The Timber Problem of the Royal Navy, 1652–1860* (Cambridge: Harvard University Press, 1926);

R. J. B. Knight, "New England Forests and British Seapower: Albion Revised," *American Neptune* 46 (1986): 221–29; and Daniel A. Baugh, ed., *Naval Administration, 1715–1750* (London: Naval Records Society, 1977), 237–54. Late in the colonial period, America's chief exports were tobacco, bread and flour, rice, dried fish, and indigo, about half of its exports going to Britain and a quarter to the West Indies. James F. Shepherd and Gary M. Walton, *Shipping, Maritime Trade, and the Economic Development of Colonial North America* (Cambridge: Cambridge University Press, 1972), 96–98.

13. These frigates were the *Falkland*, 42 cannon (1695), *Bedford Gally*, 28 (1697), *Boston*, 24 (1748), and *America*, 44 (1749). David Lyon, *The Sailing Navy List: All the Ships of the Royal Navy—Built, Purchased, and Captured—1688–1860* (London: Conway Maritime Press, 1993), 24, 27, 79, 87, 200–201, 211–12; Howard I. Chapelle, *The History of the American Sailing Navy: The Ships and Their Development* (New York: W. W. Norton, 1949), 3–51; Joseph A. Goldenberg, *Shipbuilding in Colonial America* (Charlottesville: University Press of Virginia, 1976), 108–16; Daniel A. Baugh, *Naval Administration in the Age of Walpole* (Princeton: Princeton University Press, 1965), 256–57. Very often ships carried more cannon than those of their official rating. I will consistently give the official number after the name of the ship rather than the actual number carried.

14. James Pritchard, *Louis XV's Navy, 1748–1762: A Study of Organization and Administration* (Kingston: McGill-Queen's University Press, 1987), 131; John B. Harbron, *Trafalgar and the Spanish Navy* (London: Conway Maritime Press; Annapolis: Naval Institute Press, 1988), 51–75.

15. James G. Lyndon, *Pirates, Privateers, and Profits* (Upper Saddle River NJ: Gregg Press, 1970); Benjamin W. Labaree, William M. Fowler Jr., Edward W. Sloan, John B. Hattendorf, Jeffrey J. Safford, and Andrew W. German, *America and the Sea* (Mystic

CT: Mystic Seaport, 1998), 83–84, 136; Carl E. Swanson, "American Privateering and Imperial Warfare, 1739–1748," *William and Mary Quarterly*, 3rd ser., 42 (1985): 357–82.

16. William M. Fowler Jr., *Rebels under Sail: The American Navy during the Revolution* (New York: Charles Scribner's Sons, 1976), 238–39.

17. Fowler, *Rebels under Sail*, 14, 333. For American sailors, see Daniel Vickers, *Young Men and the Sea: Yankee Seafarers in the Age of Sail* (New Haven: Yale University Press, 2005). Consult also Paolo Coletta, *American Naval History: A Guide*, 2nd ed. (Lanham MD: Scarecrow Press, 2000), a superb bibliography of books, dissertations, and articles on all of American naval history.

18. Stout, *Royal Navy in America*, 71–72, 119; Denver Brunsman, "The Knowles Impressment Riots of the 1740s," *Early American Studies* 5 (2007): 324–66; John Lax and William Pencak, "The Knowles Riot and the Crisis of the 1740s in Massachusetts," *Perspectives in American History* 10 (1976): 163–214; Jesse Lemisch, "Jack Tar in the Streets: Merchant Seamen in the Politics of Revolutionary America," *William and Mary Quarterly*, 3rd ser., 25 (1968): 371–401.

19. For the challenges of commanding a warship in battle, see Sam Willis, *Fighting at Sea in the Eighteenth Century: The Art of Sailing Warfare* (Rochester NY: Boydell Press, 2008).

20. Julian Gwyn, "The Royal Navy in North America, 1712–1776," in *The British Navy and the Use of Naval Power in the Eighteenth Century*, ed. Jeremy Black and Philip Woodfine (Atlantic Highlands NJ: Humanities Press International, 1989), 129–47; Carl E. Swanson, "'The Unspeakable Calamity this poor Province Suffers from Pyrats': South Carolina and the Golden Age of Piracy," *Northern Mariner* 21 (2011): 117–42.

21. The best account of the Cartagena expedition is Richard Harding, *Amphibious Warfare in the Eighteenth Century: The British Expedition to the West Indies, 1740–1742* (Woodbridge: Boydell

Press for the Royal Historical Society, 1991). For the 1741 attack on St. Augustine and the Spanish counterattack on Georgia, see Wright, *Anglo-Spanish Rivalry*, 90–97, and Julian Gwyn, *An Admiral for America: Sir Peter Warren, Vice Admiral of the Red, 1703–1752* (Gainesville: University Press of Florida, 2004), 29–36.

22. There is a good account of the siege in Gwyn, *An Admiral for America*, 76–99. See also John A. Schutz, *William Shirley: King's Governor of Massachusetts* (Chapel Hill: University of North Carolina Press, 1961), 85–100, and Howard Millar Chapin, "New England Vessels in the Expedition against Louisbourg, 1745," *New England Historical and Genealogical Register* 77 (1923): 59–71, 95–110. For the return of Louisbourg to France, see Jack M. Sosin, "Louisbourg and the Peace of Aix-la-Chapelle, 1748," *William and Mary Quarterly*, 3rd ser., 14 (1957): 516–35.

23. See Enid Robbie, *The Forgotten Commissioner: Sir William Mildmay and the Anglo-French Commission of 1750–1755* (East Lansing: Michigan State University Press, 2003).

24. Jonathan R. Dull, *The French Navy and the Seven Years' War* (Lincoln: University of Nebraska Press, 2005), 12–32.

25. Jonathan R. Dull, *Benjamin Franklin and the American Revolution* (Lincoln: University of Nebraska Press, 2010), 20.

26. Dull, *French Navy and the Seven Years' War*, 144–45. The best survey of the British war effort is in Daniel Baugh, *The Global Seven Years' War, 1754–1763* (Harlow UK: New York: Longman, 2011).

27. For the war on inland waters, see Russell P. Bellico, *Sail and Steam in the Mountains: A Maritime and Military History of Lake George and Lake Champlain* (Fleischmanns NY: Purple Mountain Press, 1991), 23–113; D. Peter MacLeod, "The French Siege of Oswego in 1756: Inland Naval Warfare in North America," *American Neptune* 49 (1989): 262–71; Brian Dunnigan, ed., *Memoirs on the Late War in North America between France and England by Pierre Pouchot*, trans. Michael Cardy (Youngstown NY: Old Fort Niagara Association, 1994); Lyon, *Sailing Navy List*, 297, 299.

28. The classic study is James A. Henretta, *"Salutary Neglect": Colonial Administration under the Duke of Newcastle* (Princeton: Princeton University Press, 1972). For Franklin and Britain, see Dull, *Franklin*, 17–39.

29. See Thomas Truxes, *Defying Empire: Trading with the Enemy in Colonial New York* (New Haven: Yale University Press, 2008).

30. Gwyn, "Royal Navy," 141–42; R. C. Simmons, "Trade Legislation and Its Enforcement, 1748–1776," in *Blackwell Encyclopedia of the American Revolution*, ed. Greene and Pole, 161–70; Stout, *Royal Navy in America*, 25–55; Daniel A. Baugh, "Maritime Strength and Atlantic Commerce: The Uses of 'a Great Maritime Empire,'" in *An Imperial State at War: Britain from 1689 to 1815*, ed. Lawrence Stone (London: Routledge, 1994), 185–223.

31. Stout, *Royal Navy in America*, 59, 141–43; Lyon, *Sailing Navy List*, 211–12.

32. Stout, *Royal Navy in America*, 162–63; James L. Nelson, *George Washington's Secret Navy: How the American Revolution Went to Sea* (New York: McGraw-Hill, 2008), 65–73.

TWO. THE WAR AGAINST BRITAIN

1. Dull, *Franklin*, 45.

2. James L. Nelson, *Benedict Arnold's Navy: The Ragtag Fleet That Lost the Battle of Lake Champlain but Won the American Revolution* (Camden ME: McGraw-Hill, 2006), 83; Brendan Morrissey, *Boston, 1775: The Shot Heard around the World* (New York: Osprey, 1995), 26.

3. Nelson, *George Washington's Secret Navy*, ix–xiii, 37–61, 76–78, 136–47.

4. Nelson, *Benedict Arnold's Navy*, 5–63; Bellico, *Sail and Steam in the Mountains*, 116–20; Chapelle, *American Sailing Navy*, 104–12; Paul H. Silverstone, *The Sailing Navy, 1775–1854* (Annapolis: Naval Institute Press, 2001), 16–17. For an excellent study of early American gunboats, see Spencer C. Tucker, *The Jeffersonian Gunboat Navy* (Columbia: University of South Carolina Press, 1993).

5. Nelson, *Benedict Arnold's Navy*, 64–126; Dull, *Franklin*, 54–56; Walter Nugent, *Habits of Empire: A History of American Expansion* (New York: Alfred A. Knopf, 2008).

6. Nelson, *George Washington's Secret Navy*, 93–132, 148–55, 168–76, 261–67; Fowler, *Rebels under Sail*, 39–60; Silverstone, *Sailing Navy*, 6–7, 13–14, 18–20; Christopher P. Magra, *The Fisherman's Cause: Atlantic Commerce and Maritime Dimensions of the American Revolution* (Cambridge: Cambridge University Press, 2009), 177–98; John W. Jackson, *The Pennsylvania Navy, 1775–1781: The Defense of the Delaware* (New Brunswick NJ: Rutgers University Press, 1974), 11–23. There are numerous histories of the Continental navy, the best of which is Fowler, *Rebels under Sail*, although the most detailed is still Gardner W. Allen, *A Naval History of the American Revolution* (2 vols., Boston: Houghton Mifflin, 1913). As with most periods of American naval history, much of the best work is biographical. This includes Sheldon S. Cohen, *Commodore Abraham Whipple: Privateer, Patriot, Pioneer* (Gainesville: University Press of Florida, 2010); Louis Arthur Norton, *Joshua Barney: Hero of the Revolution and the War of 1812* (Annapolis: Naval Institute Press, 2000); James L. Howard, *Seth Harding, Mariner: A Naval Picture of the Revolution* (New Haven: Yale University Press; London: Humphrey Milford, Oxford University Press, 1930); William James Morgan, *Captains to the Northward: The New England Captains in the Continental Navy* (Barre MA: Barre Gazette, 1959); Tim McGrath, *John Barry: An American Hero in the Age of Sail* (Yardley PA: Westholme, 2010), and several books by William Bell Clark, including *Lambert Wickes: Sea Raider and Diplomat: The Story of a Naval Captain of the Revolution* (New Haven: Yale University Press; London: Humphrey Milford, Oxford University Press, 1932); *Captain Dauntless: The Story of Nicholas Biddle of the Continental Navy* (Baton Rouge: Louisiana State University Press, 1949) and *Gallant John Barry, 1745–1803: The Story of a Naval Hero of Two Wars* (New York: Macmillan, 1938). The

best published documentary collections are William Bell Clark et al., eds., *Naval Documents of the American Revolution* (11 vols. to date, Washington: Government Printing Office, 1964–) and C. O. Paullin, ed., *Out-Letters of the Continental Marine Committee and Board of Admiralty: August 1776–December 1780* (2 vols., New York: De Vinne Press for the Naval Historical Society, 1914). For the state navies, see Silverstone, *Sailing Navy*, 18–20, and Robert Scheina, "A Matter of Definition: The New Jersey Navy, 1777–1783," *American Neptune* 39 (1979): 209–17. There are numerous surveys of American naval history; one of the best is Kenneth J. Hagan, *This People's Navy: The Making of American Sea Power* (New York: Free Press, 1991). Jack Sweetman, *American Naval History: An Illustrated Chronology of the U.S. Navy and Marine Corps, 1771–Present*, 3rd ed. (Annapolis: Naval Institute Press, 2002) is very useful. For the British navy, see Piers Mackesy, *The War for America, 1775–1783* (Cambridge: Harvard University Press, 1965); David Syrett, *The Royal Navy in American Waters, 1775–1783* (Aldershot: Scolar Press, 1989) and *The Royal Navy in European Waters during the American Revolutionary War* (Columbia: University of South Carolina Press, 1998); John A. Tilley, *The British Navy and the American Revolution* (Columbia: University of South Carolina Press, 1987); and W. M. James, *The British Navy in Adversity: A Study of the War of American Independence* (New York: Longmans, Green, 1926).

7. Nelson, *George Washington's Secret Navy*, 4–5, 210–23.

8. Chapelle, *American Sailing Navy*, 79–82; Silverstone, *Sailing Navy*, 2; Samuel Eliot Morison, *John Paul Jones: A Sailor's Biography* (Boston: Little, Brown, 1959), 318–30.

9. The most detailed description of the frigates is in Chapelle, *American Sailing Navy*, 52–79, 82–98, but see also Silverstone, *Sailing Navy*, 2–10; Donald L. Canney, *Sailing Warships of the U.S. Navy* (London: Chatham, 2001), 12–20; and Lyon, *Sailing Navy List*, 217–19.

10. Lyon, *Sailing Navy List*, 64–91; Dull, *French Navy and American Independence*, 352–58.

11. Lincoln Diamant, *Chaining the Hudson: The Fight for the River in the American Revolution* (New York: Carel, 1989), 115–20.

12. Jackson, *Pennsylvania Navy*, 206–208, 209–10.

13. Prizes taken by each warship of the Continental navy are listed in Silverstone, *Sailing Navy*, 2–13.

14. The best account is George E. Buker, *The Penobscot Expedition: Commodore Saltonstall and the Massachusetts Conspiracy of 1779* (Annapolis: Naval Institute Press, 2002).

15. Cohen, *Whipple*, 109–21; Carl P. Borick, *A Gallant Defense: The Siege of Charleston, 1780* (Columbia: University of South Carolina Press, 2003).

16. Dull, *Age of the Ship of the Line*, 28–29.

17. See Jean Boudriot, *John Paul Jones and the* Bonhomme Richard: *A Reconstruction of the Ship and an Account of the Battle with* HMS Serapis, trans. David H. Roberts (Annapolis: Naval Institute Press, 1987). Its crew was of mixed nationality, its naval officers were American, and its officers of marines were French: Augustus C. Buell, *Paul Jones, Founder of the American Navy: A History* (2 vols., New York: C. Scribner's Sons, 1900), 2:407–13. The best account of the battle is Thomas Schaeper, *John Paul Jones and the Battle off Flamborough Head* (New York: Peter Lang, 1989). There are numerous biographies of Jones including Morison, *Jones*; Joseph Callo, *John Paul Jones: America's First Sea Warrior* (Annapolis: Naval Institute Press, 2006); and Evan Thomas, *John Paul Jones: Sailor, Hero, Father of the American Navy* (New York: Simon & Schuster, 2003).

18. There is an excellent history of the ship, James A. Lewis, *Neptune's Militia: The Frigate* South Carolina *during the American Revolution* (Kent OH: Kent State University Press, 1999).

19. Also important were the *Independence* and *Andrew Doria*, which arrived at Philadelphia from the West Indies at the end of

1776 with blankets and vital supplies for the Continental army: David Hackett Fischer, *Washington's Crossing* (Oxford: Oxford University Press, 2004), 156. For further discussion of the merits of the Continental navy, see Jonathan R. Dull, "Was the Continental Navy a Mistake?" *American Neptune* 44 (1984): 167–70; William S. Dudley and Michael A. Palmer, "No Mistake About It: A Response to Jonathan R. Dull," *American Neptune* 45 (1985): 244–48; and George C. Daughan, *If by Sea: The Forging of the American Navy—From the American Revolution to the War of 1812* (New York: Perseus Books Group, 2008), 28–239.

20. Nelson, *George Washington's Secret Navy*; Fischer, *Washington's Crossing*, 215–20; Magra, *Fisherman's Cause*, 219–32; George Athan Billias, *General John Glover and His Marblehead Mariners* (New York: Henry Holt, 1960).

21. Nelson, *Benedict Arnold's Navy*, 220–326; John R. Bratten, *The Gondola Philadelphia and the Battle of Lake Champlain* (College Station: Texas A&M University Press, 2002); James Kirby Marine, "The Battle of Valcour Island," in *Great American Naval Battles*, ed. Jack Sweetman (Annapolis: Naval Institute Press, 1998), 3–26. For the British ships on Lake Champlain, see Lyon, *Sailing Navy List*, 298.

22. Jackson, *Pennsylvania Navy*, 95–281.

23. Ronald G. Tagney, *The World Turned Upside Down: Essex County during America's Turbulent Years, 1763–1790* (West Newbury MA: Essex County History, 1989), 397–98. See also Labaree et al., *America and the Sea*, 136; William James Morgan, "American Privateering in America's War for Independence, 1775–1783," *American Neptune* 36 (1976): 79–87; William Laird Clowes, *The Royal Navy: A History from the Earliest Times to the Present* (7 vols., Boston: Little, Brown; London: Sampson Low, Marston, 1897–1903), 3:396. Not all privateers flying the American flag were American. See William Bell Clark, *Ben Franklin's Privateers: A Naval Epic of the American Revolution* (Baton Rouge: Louisiana State University Press, 1956).

24. Although a work of popular rather than scholarly history, Robert H. Patton's *Patriot Pirates: The Privateer War for Freedom and Fortune in the American Revolution* (New York: Vintage Books, 2008) does make a serious attempt to deal with the issues raised by privateering.

25. Richard Buel Jr., *In Irons: Britain's Naval Supremacy and the American Revolutionary Economy* (New Haven: Yale University Press, 1998) is indispensable to an understanding of the war. I have discussed the war in *Age of the Ship of the Line*, 91–117, and at far greater length in *The French Navy and American Independence*. See also John Reeve, "British Naval Strategy: War on a Global Scale," and James Pritchard, "French Strategy in the American Revolution," in *Strategy in the American War of Independence: A Global Approach*, ed. Kenneth J. Hagan and Michael T. McMaster (London: Routledge, 2010), 73–99, 141–62. Secret arms purchases from France, Spain, and the Netherlands prior to their entrance into the war also were vital: Magra, *Fisherman's Cause*, 161–76.

26. Greene, *Understanding the American Revolution*, 368–69.

27. For an excellent summary, see Fowler, *Rebels under Sail*, 61–90.

THREE. A NEW NAVY FIGHTS FRANCE AND THE BARBARY STATES

1. For details, see Buel, *In Irons*.

2. The abortive negotiations to revise the preliminary treaty can be followed in detail in volume 40 of Leonard W. Labaree et al., eds., *The Papers of Benjamin Franklin* (40 vols. to date, New Haven: Yale University Press, 1959–). For a summary, see Vincent T. Harlow, *The Founding of the Second British Empire, 1763–1793* (2 vols., London: Longmans, Green, 1952–64), 1:223–311.

3. The best account of Congress's difficulties is Frederick W. Marks III, *Independence on Trial: Foreign Affairs and the Making of the Constitution* (Baton Rouge: Louisiana State University Press,

1973). Because of its republican institutions, the United States was commonly expected to remain weak and divided like the Netherlands: Jonathan R. Dull, "Two Republics in a Hostile World: The United States and the Netherlands in the 1780s," in *The American Revolution: Its Character and Limits*, ed. Jack P. Greene (New York: New York University Press, 1987), 149–63. Gordon Wood, *Empire of Liberty: A History of the Early Republic, 1789–1815* (Oxford: Oxford University Press, 2009) is an excellent survey.

4. See Charles R. Ritcheson, *Aftermath of Revolution: British Policy toward the United States, 1783–1795* (Dallas: Southern Methodist University Press, 1969). A good introduction to the diplomacy of the period is Lawrence S. Kaplan, *Colonies into Nation: American Diplomacy, 1763–1801* (New York: Macmillan; London: Collier-Macmillan, 1972).

5. European warships, such as those of the French navy or those of the Knights of Malta, in turn captured and enslaved sailors from the Barbary States. Daniel Panzac, *Barbary Corsairs: The End of a Legend, 1800–1820*, trans. Victoria Hobson (Leiden: Brill, 2005), is a superb study of the maritime activities of the Barbary States (who also engaged in normal trade). For background see also the perceptive essay "The New Atlantic: Naval Warfare in the Sixteenth Century" by the brilliant historian N. A. M. Rodger, in his *Essays in Naval History from Medieval to Modern* (Burlington VT: Ashgate, 2009).

6. There is an excellent recent study of these negotiations, Priscilla H. Roberts and Richard S. Roberts, *Thomas Barclay (1728–1793): Consul in France, Diplomat in Barbary* (Bethlehem PA: Lehigh University Press, 2008).

7. Irving H. King, *George Washington's Coast Guard: Origins of the U.S. Revenue Cutter Service, 1790–1801* (Annapolis: Naval Institute Press, 1978).

8. Michael A. Palmer, *Stoddert's War: Naval Operations during the Quasi-War with France, 1798–1801*, rev. ed. (Annapolis: Naval Institute Press, 2000), 3–4.

9. Labaree, *Papers of Benjamin Franklin*, 39:419–21. A few years later the Algerian navy contained thirteen ships carrying 218 cannon: Panzac, *Barbary Corsairs*, 48.

10. Marshall Smelser, *The Congress Founds a Navy, 1787–1798* (Notre Dame IN: Notre Dame University Press, 1959), 35–71; Craig L. Symonds, *Navalists and Antinavalists: The Naval Policy Debate in the United States, 1785–1827* (Newark: University of Delaware Press; Toronto: Associated University Press, 1980), 27–38. William M. Fowler Jr., *Jack Tars and Commodores: The American Navy, 1783–1815* (Boston: Houghton Mifflin, 1984) is a useful survey of the postwar period. See also Michael J. Crawford and Christine F. Hughes, *The Reestablishment of the Navy, 1787–1801: Historical Overview and Select Bibliography* (Washington DC: Department of Defense, 1995).

11. Chapelle, *American Sailing Navy*, 119–34; Canney, *Sailing Warships*, 23–48. For their construction see also Geoffrey M. Footner, *USS* Constellation: *From Frigate to Sloop of War* (Annapolis: Naval Institute Press, 2003), 1–31, and Ian W. Toll, *Six Frigates: The Epic History of the Founding of the U.S. Navy* (New York: W. W. Norton, 2006), 44–62, 72–77, 95–98. For the *Constitution*, see also Tyrone Martin, *A Most Fortunate Ship: A Narrative History of Old Ironsides*, rev. ed. (Annapolis: Naval Institute Press, 2003).

12. See Lyon, *Sailing Navy List*, 76, 270, for a comparison of the *Panther* and the *President* (which was captured by the British at the end of the War of 1812).

13. Rif Winfield, *British Warships in the Age of Sail, 1793–1817: Construction, Careers, and Fates* (London: Chatham; St. Paul: MBI, 2005), 132–33; Alain Demerliac, *La Marine de la Révolution: Nomenclature des navires français de 1792 à 1799* (Nice: Editions Omega, 1999), 66–67; Robert Gardiner, *Frigates of the Napoleonic Wars* (Annapolis: Naval Institute Press, 2000), 40–48; Jean Boudriot, *The History of the French Frigate, 1650–1850*, trans. David H. Roberts (Rotheford UK: Jean Boudriot, 1993), 227–50. For the *Serapis*, see Lyon, *Sailing Navy List*, 82–83.

14. Chapelle, *American Sailing Navy*, 130; Palmer, *Stoddert's War*, 28; Thomas C. Gillmer, *Old Ironsides: The Rise, Decline, and Resurrection of the* USS Constitution (Camden ME: International Marine, 1993); N. A. M. Rodger, *The Command of the Ocean: A Naval History of Britain, 1649–1815* (London: Allen Lane, 2004), 414.

15. Smelser, *Congress Founds the Navy*, 72–86; Symonds, *Navalists and Antinavalists*, 39–50.

16. Silverstone, *Sailing Navy*, 26–30; Chapelle, *American Sailing Navy*, 135–40.

17. Alexander De Conde, *Entangling Alliance: Politics and Diplomacy under George Washington* (Durham: Duke University Press, 1958), 354, 400–402. There are a number of excellent books on the politics and diplomacy of the 1790s. For relations with France during the decade, see De Conde, *Entangling Alliance* and its sequel, *The Quasi-War: The Politics and Diplomacy of the Undeclared War with France, 1797–1801* (New York: Charles Scribner's Sons, 1966), as well as Albert Hall Bowman, *The Struggle for Neutrality: Franco-American Diplomacy during the Federalist Era* (Knoxville: University of Tennessee Press, 1974). Books on relations with Britain include Ritcheson, *Aftermath of Revolution*; Jerald Combs, *The Jay Treaty: Political Battleground of the Founding Fathers* (Berkeley: University of California Press, 1970); and Bradford Perkins, *The First Rapprochement: England and the United States, 1795–1805* (Philadelphia: University of Pennsylvania Press, 1955).

18. De Conde, *Entangling Alliance*, 270–83; Bowman, *Struggle for Neutrality*, 84–90; Harry Ammon, *The Genet Mission* (New York: W. W. Norton, 1973), 120–26. The French also outfitted privateers in American ports, particularly Charleston: Melvin H. Jackson, *Privateers in Charleston, 1793–1796* (Washington DC: Smithsonian Institution Press, 1969).

19. De Conde, *Entangling Alliance*, 92–94; Bowman, *Struggle for Neutrality*, 128n, 143–44.

20. De Conde, *Entangling Alliance*, 305, 402–404; Bowman,

Struggle for Neutrality, 159–63; Dull, *Age of the Ship of the Line,* 135–36.

21. De Conde, *Entangling Alliance,* 434, 437. For British operations in the West Indies, see Michael Duffy, *Soldiers, Sugar, and Seapower: The British Expeditions to the West Indies and the War against Revolutionary France* (Oxford: Clarendon Press, 1987).

22. Perkins, *First Rapprochement,* 47–48, 65, 70–75, 82. As a further benefit, the fear of an American alliance with Britain led Spain to make a treaty with the United States conceding to it navigation of the Mississippi River, the right to deposit goods at New Orleans, and a favorable Florida boundary settlement: John Kukla, *A Wilderness So Immense: The Louisiana Purchase and the Destiny of America* (New York: Alfred A. Knopf, 2003), 179–94; Samuel Flagg Bemis, *Pinckney's Treaty: America's Advantage from Europe's Distress, 1783–1800,* rev. ed. (New Haven: Yale University Press, 1960).

23. Ulane Bonnel, *La France, les Etats-Unis, et la guerre de course (1797–1815)* (Paris: Nouvelles Editions Latines, 1961), 319–67.

24. The best study of the negotiations is William Stinchcombe, *The XYZ Affair* (Westport CT: Greenwood Press, 1980).

25. See particularly Smelser, *Congress Founds the Navy,* 124–77, and Symonds, *Navalists and Antinavalists,* 51–72.

26. Palmer, *Stoddert's War* is an excellent account of Stoddert's accomplishments as well as naval operations during the hostilities. It is largely based on Dudley W. Knox, ed., *Naval Documents Related to the Quasi-War with France: Naval Operations, February 1797–December 1801* (7 vols., Washington DC: Government Printing Office, 1935–38). See also Symonds, *Navalists and Antinavalists,* 72–86, and Christopher McKee, *A Gentlemanly and Honorable Profession: The Creation of the U.S. Naval Officer Corps, 1794–1815* (Annapolis: Naval Institute Press, 1991), 6–7, 46–47.

27. For the American warships, see Silverstone, *Sailing Navy,* 26–35, 38, 45, 50, 79–80; Chapelle, *American Sailing Navy,* 115–78;

Canney, *Sailing Warships,* 49–58; Frederick C. Leiner, *Millions for Defense: The Subscription Warships of 1798* (Annapolis: Naval Institute Press, 2000); and Philip Chadwick Foster Smith, *The Frigate Essex Papers: Building the Salem Frigate, 1798–1799* (Salem MA: Peabody Museum of Salem, 1974). For the French frigates, see Palmer, *Stoddert's War,* 71, 148–49; Bonnel, *La France, les Etats-Unis, et la guerre de course,* 104; Demerliac, *La Marine de la Révolution,* 35, 67–70, 72–73; and David F. Long, *Ready to Hazard: A Biography of Commodore William Bainbridge, 1774–1833* (Hanover NH: University Press of New England, 1981), 28.

28. Palmer, *Stoddert's War,* 98–103, 185–88; Toll, *Six Frigates,* 114–20, 132–35; Eugene S. Ferguson, *Truxtun of the Constellation: The Life of Commodore Thomas Truxtun, U.S. Navy, 1755–1822,* rev. ed. (Baltimore: Johns Hopkins University Press, 2000), 160–78, 187–202; Bowman, *Struggle for Neutrality,* 343, 345–49. The *Insurgente* was taken into the American navy, but the following year it was lost in a storm with all hands.

29. Fowler, *Jack Tars and Commodores,* 50–53; Palmer, *Stoddert's War,* 151–65; Thomas O. Ott, *The Haitian Revolution, 1789–1804* (Knoxville: University of Tennessee Press, 1973), 114; Philippe R. Girard, "Black Talleyrand: Toussaint Louverture's Diplomacy, 1789–1802," *William & Mary Quarterly,* 3rd ser., 66 (2009): 109–10, 112; Linda M. Maloney, *The Captain from Connecticut: The Life and Naval Times of Isaac Hull* (Boston: Northeastern University Press, 1986), 29–52, 56–57. Maloney's biography is marvelous.

30. The unsuccessful negotiations to avert war are discussed in Robert J. Allison, *The Crescent Obscured: The United States and the Muslim World, 1776–1815* (New York: Oxford University Press, 1995), 153–85, an exceptionally sophisticated and objective book.

31. Panzac, *Barbary Corsairs,* 277–80.

32. There are numerous naval histories of the war. They tend to be good at describing the obstacles faced by the Americans and their courage in facing them, but not very good at treating

the enemy as people. Glenn Tucker's *The Barbary Wars and the Birth of the U.S. Navy* (Indianapolis: Bobbs-Merrill, 1963) uses the usual stereotypes but is very detailed and entertaining. Maloney, *Captain from Connecticut*, 61–114; Long, *Ready to Hazard*, 67–102; Christopher McKee, *Edward Preble: A Naval Biography, 1761–1807* (Annapolis: Naval Institute Press, 1972); and Louis B. Wright, *The First Americans in North Africa: William Eaton's Struggle for a Vigorous Policy against the Barbary Pirates, 1799–1805* (Princeton: Princeton University Press, 1945) are useful. For a documentary record, see Dudley W. Knox, ed., *Naval Documents Related to the United States Wars with the Barbary Pirates: Naval Operations Including Diplomatic Background, 1785–1807* (6 vols., Washington: Government Printing Office, 1939–44).

33. Robert J. Allison, *Stephen Decatur: American Naval Hero, 1779–1820* (Amherst: University of Massachusetts Press, 2005), 47–54.

34. Toll, *Six Frigates*, 224; Fowler, *Jack Tars and Commodores*, 124; Perkins, *First Rapprochement*, 153–54.

FOUR. A PRECARIOUS NEUTRALITY ENDS IN A SECOND WAR

1. Dull, *Age of the Ship of the Line*, 161–62; Conor Cruise O'Brien, *The Long Affair: Thomas Jefferson and the French Revolution, 1785–1800* (Chicago: University of Chicago Press, 1996), 280–93; Tim Matthewson, "Jefferson and Haiti," *Journal of Southern History* 61 (1995): 209–48.

2. For the naval dimensions of the Louisiana crisis, see Alexander De Conde, *This Affair of Louisiana* (New York: Charles Scribner's Sons, 1976), 198, 220, 229; Kukla, *A Wilderness So Immense*, 227–29. De Conde's superbly researched book is a reliable guide to the diplomacy and politics of the Louisiana Purchase, while Kukla's book covers the same ground a little less thoroughly but provides interesting background material. For a provocative analysis of Jefferson's policies, see Michael Zuckerman, *Almost*

Chosen People: Oblique Biographies in the American Grain (Berkeley: University of California Press, 1993), 175–218.

3. American relations with Britain are detailed in three brilliant books: Bradford Perkins, *Prologue to War: England and the United States, 1805–1812* (Berkeley: University of California Press, 1961); Burton Spivak, *Jefferson's English Crisis: Commerce, Embargo, and the Republican Revolution* (Charlottesville: University Press of Virginia, 1979); and J. C. A. Stagg, *Mr. Madison's War: Politics, Diplomacy, and Warfare in the Early American Republic, 1783–1830* (Princeton: Princeton University Press, 1983), 3–176. For relations with France see Bonnel, *La France, les Etats-Unis, et la guerre de course,* 152–313, 374–407, 421–25; Clifford Egan, *Neither Peace nor War: Franco-American Relations, 1803–1812* (Baton Rouge: Louisiana State University Press, 1983); and Peter P. Hill, *Napoleon's Troublesome Americans: Franco-American Relations, 1804–1815* (Washington DC: Potomac Books, 2005).

4. James Fulton Zimmerman, *Impressment of American Seamen* (New York: Columbia University Press, 1925), 255.

5. Silverstone, *Sailing Navy*, 46–47. See also Chapelle, *American Sailing Navy*, 182–88, 210–16.

6. Tucker, *Jeffersonian Gunboat Navy*, 102; Chapelle, *American Sailing Navy*, 151–54, 189–210; Silverstone, *Sailing Navy*, 27–59. See also Gene A. Smith, *For the Purposes of Defense: The Politics of the Jeffersonian Gunboat Program* (Newark: University of Delaware Press, 1995). A handful of 3-gun and 4-gun bomb ketches were built or purchased between 1804 and 1806, and almost $3 million was spent on harbor and coastal fortifications in the expectation that anything more than local attacks would be deterred by financial and logistical obstacles: Donald R. Hickey, *The War of 1812: A Forgotten Conflict* (Urbana: University of Illinois Press, 1989), 8; Emanuel Ray Lewis, *Seacoast Fortifications of the United States: An Introductory History* (Washington DC: Smithsonian Institution Press, 1970), 21–36.

7. Spencer C. Tucker and Frank T. Reuter, *Injured Honor: The Chesapeake-Leopard Affair, June 22, 1807* (Annapolis: Naval Institute Press, 1996).

8. Spivak, *Jefferson's English Crisis*, 77, 97; Perkins, *Prologue to War*, 149–56.

9. Stagg, *Mr. Madison's War*, 36–47.

10. Perkins, *Prologue to War*, 323–40; Stagg, *Mr. Madison's War*, 7. See also Timothy D. Willig, *Restoring the Chain of Friendship: British Policy and the Indians of the Great Lakes, 1783–1815* (Lincoln: University of Nebraska Press, 2008).

11. Possibly even naval victories. According to newspaper accounts, Napoleon, in addition to preparing to invade Russia, was undertaking a European-wide shipbuilding program. There is no evidence, however, that President Madison took the French naval threat to Britain seriously. In spite of British concern, the shipbuilding program posed little danger: Dull, *Age of the Ship of the Line*, 173; Richard Glover, "The French Fleet, 1807–14: Britain's Problem and Madison's Opportunity," *Journal of Modern History* 39 (1967): 233–52. Americans believed their main hope of winning an easy victory was in invading Canada.

12. Silverstone, *Sailing Navy*, 26–34.

13. Figures are for July 1812 and count only ships of the fifth rate as frigates: Wade G. Dudley, *Splintering the Wooden Wall: The British Blockade of the United States, 1812–1815* (Annapolis: Naval Institute Press, 2003), 39.

14. Histories of the war written predominantly from an American perspective include Stagg, *Mr. Madison's War*, Hickey, *War of 1812*, Dudley, *Splintering the Wooden Wall*, Fowler, *Jack Tars and Commodores*, 162–260, Donald R. Hickey and Donald E. Graves, *Don't Give Up the Ship: Myths of the War of 1812* (Chicago: University of Chicago Press, 2006), John K. Mahon, *The War of 1812* (Gainesville: University of Florida Press, 1972), and Stephen Budiansky, *Perilous Fight: America's Intrepid War with Britain on the*

High Seas, 1812–1815 (New York: Alfred A. Knopf, 2010). J. Mackay Hitsman, *The Incredible War of 1812: A Military History* (rev. ed., Toronto: Robin Brass Studio, 1999) is written from a Canadian perspective, while Jon Latimer, *1812: War with America* (Cambridge: Belknap Press of Harvard University Press, 2007), Jeremy Black, *The War of 1812 in the Age of Napoleon* (Norman: University of Oklahoma Press, 2009), and Robert Gardiner, ed., *The Naval War of 1812* (London: Chatham, 1998) are written from a British perspective. Alan Taylor, *The Civil War of 1812: American Citizens, British Subjects, Irish Rebels, and Indian Allies* (New York: Alfred A. Knopf, 2010) is a brilliant analysis of the brutal war along the American-Canadian border. William S. Dudley et al., *The Naval War of 1812: A Documentary History* (3 vols. to date, Washington DC: Naval History Center, 1985–) is a superb collection of documents.

15. Graham, *Empire of the North Atlantic*, 246–47.

16. McKee's *Gentlemanly and Honorable Profession*, perhaps the best book ever written about the early American navy, discusses the process by which the best officers rose to the top; see 153, 159, 165–67 for Truxtun's importance. For Preble see McKee, *Edward Preble* and "Edward Preble and the 'Boys': The Officer Corps of 1812 Revisited," in *Command under Sail: Makers of the American Naval Tradition, 1775–1850*, ed. James C. Bradford (Annapolis: Naval Institute Press, 1985), 71–96.

17. Dudley, *Splintering the Wooden Wall*, 76; Dull, *French Navy and the Seven Years' War*, 35–36, 38; John H. Schroeder, *Commodore John Rodgers: Paragon of the Early American Navy* (Gainesville: University Press of Florida, 2006), 111–18; Peter J. Kastor, "Toward 'the Maritime War Only': The Question of Naval Mobilization, 1811–1812," *Journal of Military History* 61 (1997): 455–80; Jeff Seiken, "'To Strike a Blow in the World That Shall Resound through the Universe': American Naval Operations and Options at the Start of the War of 1812," in *New Interpretations in Naval*

History: Selected Papers from the Fourteenth Naval History Symposium, ed. Randy Carol Balano and Craig L. Symonds (Annapolis: Naval Institute Press, 2001), 133–46. Not all the British were fooled by Rodgers: see Budiansky, *Perilous Fight*, 150–51.

18. Maloney, *Captain from Connecticut*, 183–200; Spencer Tucker, *Stephen Decatur: A Life Most Bold and Daring* (Annapolis: Naval Institute Press, 2005), 114–19; Long, *Ready to Hazard*, 142–66. Lyon, *Sailing Navy List*, 121–22, 270–72, gives particulars of an American 44-gun frigate and the three British 38's. Also celebrated was the later valiant fight of Captain David Porter of the *Essex* against H. M. S. *Phoebe*, 36, and *Cherub*, 26. See David F. Long, *Nothing Too Daring: A Biography of Commodore David Porter, 1780–1843* (Annapolis: Naval Institute Press, 1970), 57–174, for the lengthy cruise and final battle of the *Essex*.

19. See Hickey, *War of 1812*, 151, for the number of frigates and smaller ships. The ships of the line on the North American station or at Newfoundland were the *San Domingo, Dragon, Ramillies, Poictiers, Marlborough, Valiant, Hogue, Victorious, Plantagenet, Sceptre*, and *Bellerophon* of 74 cannon each, and the *Majestic*, 58: National Archives of the United Kingdom (formerly Public Record Office), Kew, England, Admiralty Series 8, vol. 100.

20. Dudley, *Splintering the Wooden Wall*, 33–34; Footner, *USS Constellation*, 84–98.

21. McKee, *Gentlemanly and Honorable Profession*, 9–13; Kevin D. McCranie, "Waging Protracted Naval War: The Strategic Leadership of Secretary of the U.S. Navy William Jones in the War of 1812," *Northern Mariner* 21 (2011): 143–57; Frank L. Owlsley Jr., "William Jones," in *American Secretaries of the Navy*, ed. Paolo Coletta (2 vols., Annapolis: Naval Institute Press, 1988), 1:101–12; Edward K. Eckert, "William Jones: Mr. Madison's Secretary of the Navy," *Pennsylvania Magazine of History and Biography* 96 (1972): 167–82, and *The Navy Department in the War of 1812* (Gainesville: University of Florida Press, 1973).

22. See Gardiner, *Naval War of 1812*, 65–71, and Jerome R. Garitee, *The Republic's Private Navy: The American Privateering Business as Practiced by Baltimore during the War of 1812* (Middletown CT: Wesleyan University Press, 1977). More than 10 percent of the 1,500 prizes taken from the British (excluding those recaptured) were made by the navy: Dudley, *Splintering the Wooden Wall*, 138; Silverstone, *Sailing Navy*, 26–34, 39–40, 46–47, 58–59; Spencer Tucker, *Arming the Fleet: U.S. Naval Ordnance in the Muzzle-Loading Era* (Annapolis: Naval Institute Press, 1989), 135; Stephen F. Duffy, *Captain Blakely and the* Wasp: *The Cruise of 1814* (Annapolis: Naval Institute Press, 2001); Ira Dye, *The Fatal Cruise of the* Argus: *Two Captains in the War of 1812* (Annapolis: Naval Institute Press, 1994).

23. See Dudley, *Splintering the Wooden Wall*, 145–48; Lance E. Davis and Stanley Engerman, *Naval Blockades in Peace and War: An Economic History since 1750* (Cambridge: Cambridge University Press, 2006), 98–104; C. J. Bartlett, *Great Britain and Sea Power, 1815–1853* (Oxford: Clarendon Press, 1963), 74n. The total number of British ships serving in North American waters at one time or another during the war included twenty-eight ships of the line, one 50-gun ship, and forty-eight frigates: Winfield, *British Warships in the Age of Sail*, 33, 37, 39, 41, 54–55, 60–62, 65–66, 68, 75–82, 99–102, 121, 128–30, 133–34, 140–41, 144–46, 149–50, 154–56, 159–61, 163, 165–66, 168–81, 183–86, 194–95, 198, 213, 216.

24. Eckert, *Navy Department*, 18–22, 30–31, 49–50; Claude G. Berube and John A. Rodgaard, *A Call to the Sea: Captain Charles Stewart of the Constitution* (Washington DC: Potomac Books, 2005), 75; Jeff Seiken, "'To Obtain Control of the Lakes': The United States and the Contest for Lakes Erie and Ontario," in *The Sixty Years' War for the Great Lakes, 1754–1814*, ed. David Curtis Skaggs and Larry L. Nelson (East Lansing: Michigan State University Press, 2001), 353–71; Paul A. C. Koistinen, *Beating Plowshares into Swords:*

The Political Economy of American Warfare, 1606–1865 (Lawrence: University Press of Kansas, 1996), 68.

25. The war on Lake Ontario is the subject of two superb books by Robert Malcomson, *Lords of the Lake: The Naval War on Lake Ontario, 1812–1814* (Toronto: Robin Brass Studio, 1998) and *Capital in Flames: The American Attack on York, 1813* (Montreal: Robin Brass Studio; Annapolis: Naval Institute Press, 2008). For the war on Lake Huron, see Barry Gough, *Fighting Sail on Lake Huron and Georgian Bay* (Annapolis: Naval Institute Press, 2002), and for ships on the lakes, see Lyon, *Sailing Navy List*, 297–302, Robert Malcomson, *Warships of the Great Lakes, 1754–1834* (London: Chatham, 2001), and Winfield, *British Warships in the Age of Sail*, 13. Taylor, *Civil War of 1812*, 392–402, criticizes Chauncey for lack of cooperation with the American army.

26. Robert Malcomson and Thomas Malcomson, *HMS Detroit: The Battle for Lake Erie* (St. Catharines, Ontario: Vanwell, 1990); David Curtis Skaggs and Gerald T. Altoff, *A Signal Victory: The Lake Erie Campaign, 1812–1813* (Annapolis: Naval Institute Press, 1997); Lawrence J. Friedman and David Curtis Skaggs, "Jesse Duncan Elliott and the Battle of Lake Erie: The Issue of Mental Stability," *Journal of the Early Republic* 10 (1990): 493–516; Gerald T. Altoff, *Deep Water Sailors, Shallow Water Soldiers: Manning the United States Fleet on Lake Erie, 1813* (Put-in-Bay OH: Perry Group, 1993); Davis Curtis Skaggs, *Oliver Hazard Perry: Honor, Courage, and Patriotism in the Early U.S. Navy* (Annapolis: Naval Institute Press, 2006), 49–119; Craig L. Symonds, *Decision at Sea: Five Naval Battles That Shaped American History* (New York: Oxford University Press, 2005), 23–80.

27. Latimer, *1812*, 184–92; John Sugden, *Tecumseh's Last Stand* (Norman: University of Oklahoma Press, 1985).

28. Dudley, *Splintering the Wooden Wall*, 79–109.

29. Latimer, *1812*, 301–33; Dudley, *Splintering the Wooden Wall*, 110–30; Anthony S. Pitch, *The Burning of Washington: The British*

Invasion of 1814 (Annapolis: Naval Institute Press, 1998); Daniel G. Shomette, *Flotilla: Battle for the Patuxent* (Solomons MD: Calvert Marine Museum Press, 1981); Scott S. Sheads, *The Rocket's Red Glare: The Maritime Defense of Baltimore in 1814* (Centreville MD: Tidewater, 1986); Roger Morriss, *Cockburn and the British Navy in Transition: Admiral Sir George Cockburn, 1772–1853* (Exeter: Exeter University Press, 1997), 96–114.

30. Latimer, *1812*, 345–60; Fowler, *Jack Tars and Commodores*, 230–40; David Curtis Skaggs, *Thomas Macdonough: Master of Command in the Early U.S. Navy* (Annapolis: Naval Institute Press, 2003), 83–113; Allan S. Everest, *The War of 1812 in the Champlain Valley* (Syracuse: Syracuse University Press, 1981), 141–92; David G. Fitz-Enz, *Final Invasion: Plattsburgh, the War of 1812's Most Decisive Battle* (Lincoln: University of Nebraska Press, 2009).

31. The best account of the negotiations is Bradford Perkins, *Castlereagh and Adams: England and the United States, 1812–1823* (Berkeley: University of California Press, 1964), 39–144, but see also Fred L. Engelman, *The Peace of Christmas Eve* (New York: Harcourt, Brace & World, 1962), and Samuel Flagg Bemis, *John Quincy Adams and the Foundations of American Foreign Policy* (New York: Alfred A. Knopf, 1949), 196–220.

32. Latimer, *1812*, 369–88, 402; Perkins, *Castlereagh and Adams*, 121–22, 140–42; Toll, *Six Frigates*, 442–45, 447–51; Berube and Rodgaard, *Call to the Sea*, 88–91; Lyon, *Sailing Navy List*, 129, 137; William S. Dudley, "'Old Ironsides' Last Battle: USS *Constitution* versus HM Ships *Cyane* and *Levant*," and Andrew Lambert, "Taking the *President*: HMS *Enymion* and the USS *President*," in *Fighting at Sea: Naval Battles from the Age of Sail and Steam*, ed. Douglas M. McLean ([Montreal]: Robin Brass Studio, 2008), 55–85, 86–127; Robert V. Remini, *The Battle of New Orleans* (New York: Viking, 2009).

33. Lawrence S. Kaplan, *Entangling Alliances with None: American Foreign Policy in the Age of Jefferson* (Kent OH: Kent State

University Press, 1987), 139–59; Hickey, *War of 1812*, 181, 287; Perkins, *Castlereagh and Adams*, 65.

34. See Dull, *French Navy and the Seven Years' War*, 162–70, 191–206, 228–44.

35. Eckert, *Navy Department*, 18–22, 30–31, 49–50.

36. Maloney, *Captain from Connecticut*, 432–33; Spencer C. Tucker, *Andrew Foote: Civil War Admiral on Western Waters* (Annapolis: Naval Institute Press, 2000), 20; Donald L. Canney, *Lincoln's Navy: The Ships, Men, and Organization, 1861–65* (London: Conway Maritime Press, 1998), 40–52.

37. Chapelle, *American Sailing Navy*, 305–307; Allison, *Stephen Decatur*, 186–99; Long, *Porter*, 175–80; Schroeder, *Rodgers*, 143–63; Maloney, *Captain from Connecticut*, 262–71, 278; Henry Sprout and Margaret Sprout, *The Rise of American Naval Power, 1776–1915* (Princeton: Princeton University Press, 1939), 92–93. Because the secretary of the navy was not a member of the board, it differed from the British Board of Admiralty, whose first lord was first among equals, even though he also was a cabinet member and spoke for the navy in Parliament: see C. I. Hamilton, *Anglo-French Naval Rivalry, 1840–1870* (Oxford: Clarendon Press, 1993), 252–56, a book of exceptional insight, clarity, and breadth of coverage. For a detailed study of the evolution of the Admiralty, see Hamilton's superb *The Making of the Modern Admiralty: British Naval Policy Making, 1805–1927* (Cambridge: Cambridge University Press, 2011).

38. Richard Buel Jr., *America on the Brink: How the War of 1812 Almost Destroyed the Young Republic* (New York: Palgrave Macmillan, 2005).

FIVE. TRADE PROTECTION AND WAR WITH MEXICO

1. Silverstone, *Sailing Navy*, 23–24, 35–36, 39–40; Canney, *Sailing Warships*, 61–63, 87–95, 123–29; Chapelle, *American Sailing Navy*, 255–64, 283–86, 303–304. The construction program

passed in two bills at the beginning of 1813 was for four 74-gun ships of the line, six frigates, and six sloops: Symonds, *Navals and Antinavalists,* 171–84.

2. Panzac, *Barbary Corsairs,* 260–71; Allison, *Stephen Decatur,* 160–76; Long, *Ready to Hazard,* 188–206; Frederick C. Leiner, *The End of Barbary Terror: America's 1815 War against the Pirates of North Africa* (Oxford: Oxford University Press, 2006), 39–150; Charles Lee Lewis, *David Glasgow Farragut* (2 vols., Annapolis: United States Naval Institute, 1941–43), 1:117–19.

3. Leiner: *End of Barbary Terror,* 151–76; Bartlett, *Great Britain and Sea Power,* 61–64.

4. Symonds, *Navalists and Antinavalists,* 194–218; Silverstone, *Sailing Navy,* 24–26, 36–38; Canney, *Sailing Warships,* 64–81, 95–113, 129–39; Chapelle, *American Sailing Navy,* 309–20, 324; Bartlett, *Great Britain and Sea Power,* 33–37; Jeffrey M. Dorwart and Jean K. Wolf, *The Philadelphia Navy Yard: From the Birth of the U.S. Navy to the Nuclear Age* (Philadelphia: University of Pennsylvania Press, 2001), 61–72. The French navy also delayed construction on a number of ships of the line, completing them after a considerable length of time: Alain Demerliac, *Nomenclature des navires français de 1800 à 1815: La Marine du Consulat et du Premier Empire* (Nice: Editions ANCRE, 2003), 67, 78.

5. Bartlett, *Great Britain and Sea Power,* 71–72, 342; Jan Glete, *Navies and Nations: Warships, Navies, and State Building in Europe and America, 1500–1860* (2 vols., Stockholm: Almqvist & Wiksell International, 1993), 2:451, 554–56; Andrew Lambert, *The Last Sailing Battlefleet: Maintaining Naval Mastery, 1815–1850* (London: Conway Maritime Press, 1991); Claude H. Hall, *Abel Parker Upshur, Conservative Virginian, 1790–1844* (Madison: State Historical Society of Wisconsin, 1963), 127; David Lyon and Rif Winfield, *The Sail and Steam List: All the Ships of the Royal Navy, 1815–1889* (London: Chatham, 2004).

6. John M. Belohlavek, *"Let the Eagle Soar!" The Foreign Policy of*

Andrew Jackson (Lincoln: University of Nebraska Press, 1985), 140–50; John H. Schroeder, *Matthew Calbraith Perry: Antebellum Sailor and Diplomat* (Annapolis: Naval Institute Press, 2001), 65–66.

7. Glete, *Navies and Nations*, 2:453–56, 580–81, 656–57, 669–70. American leaders well recognized the navy's inferiority in number of ships: Frederick Merk, *The Oregon Question: Essays in Anglo-American Diplomacy and Politics* (Cambridge: Belknap Press of Harvard University Press, 1967), 347–49. For naval developments during the period, see Lawrence Sondhaus, *Naval Warfare, 1815–1914* (London: Routledge, 2001).

8. For the period between the War of 1812 and the Civil War, see Daniel Walker Howe, *What Hath God Wrought: The Transformation of America, 1815–1848* (Oxford: Oxford University Press, 2007); Walter A. McDougall, *Throes of Democracy: The American Civil War Era* (New York: HarperCollins, 2008), 1–397, and *Freedom Just Around the Corner*, 419–513; Sean Wilentz, *The Rise of American Democracy: Jefferson to Lincoln* (New York: W. W. Norton, 2005). George C. Herring, *From Colony to Superpower: U.S. Foreign Relations since 1776* (Oxford: Oxford University Press, 2008), 134–223, and Howard Jones, *Crucible of Power: A History of Foreign Relations to 1913* (Wilmington DE: Scholarly Resources, 2002), 89–187, are good introductions to foreign relations between 1815 and 1861.

9. The British navy's difficulties in finding adequate funds and sailors is a central theme of Bartlett, *Great Britain and Sea Power*; yearly totals of both are given on 339–40.

10. Perkins, *Castlereagh and Adams*, 288–94; J. C. A. Stagg, *Borderlines in Borderlands: James Madison and the Spanish-American Frontier, 1776–1821* (New Haven: Yale University Press, 2009), 198–99; William Earl Weeks, *John Quincy Adams and American Global Empire* (Lexington: University Press of Kentucky, 1992), 110–11, 139–45; Frank Lawrence Owsley Jr. and Gene A. Smith, *Filibusters and Expansionists: Jeffersonian Manifest Destiny, 1800–1821* (Tuscaloosa: University of Alabama Press, 1997), 141–63.

11. Perkins, *Castlereagh and Adams*, 240–82; Samuel Flagg Bemis, *John Quincy Adams*, 278–300; Kenneth Bourne, *Britain and the Balance of Power in North America, 1815–1908* (London: Longmans, Green, 1967), 3–32.

12. Weeks, *John Quincy Adams*, 119–75; Stagg, *Borderlines in Borderlands*, 97–98, 115–22, 169–209; Bemis, *John Quincy Adams*, 317–41.

13. Herring, *From Colony to Superpower*, 154–57; Perkins, *Castlereagh and Adams*, 305–47; Ernest R. May, *The Making of the Monroe Doctrine* (Cambridge: Harvard University Press, 1975); Paul W. Schroeder, *The Transformation of European Politics, 1763–1848* (Oxford: Clarendon Press, 1994), 628–35, 665.

14. Belohlavek, *Foreign Policy of Jackson*, 53–73.

15. Howard Jones, *To the Webster-Ashburton Treaty: A Study in Anglo-American Relations, 1783–1843* (Chapel Hill: University of North Carolina Press, 1977); Howard Jones and Donald Rakestraw, *Prologue to Manifest Destiny: Anglo-American Relations in the 1840s* (Wilmington DE: Scholarly Resources, 1997), 1–150; Kenneth R. Stevens, *Border Diplomacy: The Caroline and MacLeod Affairs in Anglo-American–Canadian Relations, 1837–1842* (Tuscaloosa: University of Alabama Press, 1989); Rebecca Berens Matzke, *Deterrence through Strength: British Naval Power and Foreign Policy under Pax Britannica* (Lincoln: University of Nebraska Press, 2011), 65–84, 88–103; Francis M. Carroll, *A Good and Wise Measure: The Search for the Canadian-American Boundary, 1783–1842* (Toronto: University of Toronto Press, 2001). For George Hamilton-Gordon, Earl of Aberdeen, see Schroeder, *Transformation of European Politics*, 774, and Bartlett, *Great Britain and Sea Power*, 148–49.

16. Belohlavek, *Foreign Policy of Jackson*, 90–126.

17. See Symonds, *Navalists and Antinavalists*, 219–37.

18. Paolo E. Coletta, *The American Naval Heritage in Brief* (2nd ed., Washington DC: University Press of America, 1980), 114–19, and *American Secretaries of the Navy*, 1:123–71. For one of the better

secretaries, see Michael Birkner, *Samuel L. Southard: Jeffersonian Whig* (Rutherford NJ: Farleigh Dickinson University Press; Toronto: Associated University Presses, 1984).

19. Morriss, *Cockburn*, 242; Bartlett, *Great Britain and Sea Power*, 197–98, 213; Chapelle, *American Sailing Navy*, 308, 414–25; Sprout and Sprout, *Rise of American Naval Power*, 111–13; Silverstone, *Sailing Navy*, 72–73, 76–77; Schroeder, *Rodgers*, 200–208, and *Perry*, 78–82; Cynthia Owen Philip, *Robert Fulton: A Biography* (New York: Franklin Watts, 1985), 324–30, 345–46, 349–50; K. Jack Bauer and Stephen S. Roberts, *Register of Ships of the U.S. Navy, 1775–1990: Major Combatants* (Westport CT: Greenwood Press, 1991), 53; Ron Field, *Confederate Ironclad vs. Union Ironclad: Hampton Roads, 1862* (Oxford: Osprey, 2008), 4–6. The navy also acquired two 1-gun and one 3-gun steam-powered support ships between 1822 and 1840. For an introduction to the evolution of warships during the period, see Robert Gardiner and Andrew Lambert, *Steam, Steel, and Shellfire: The Steam Warship, 1815–1905* (London: Conway Maritime Press, 1992).

20. The best introductions to the navy's role are John H. Schroeder, *Shaping a Maritime Empire: The Commercial and Diplomatic Role of the American Navy, 1829–1861* (Westport CT: Greenwood Press, 1985) and David F. Long, *Gold Braid and Foreign Relations: Diplomatic Activities of U.S. Naval Officers, 1798–1883* (Annapolis: Naval Institute Press, 1988), 54–320. Also useful are biographies of some of the leading ship captains of the period, many of which are published in the excellent Library of Naval Biography series published by the Naval Institute Press. See, for example, Maloney, *Captain from Connecticut*, Berube and Rodgaard, *Call to the Sea*, Schroeder, *Rodgers* and *Perry*, David F. Long, *Sailor-Diplomat: A Biography of Commodore James Biddle, 1783–1848* (Boston: Northeastern University Press, 1983), Long, *Nothing Too Daring* and *Ready to Hazard*, James H. Ellis, *Mad Jack Percival: Legend of the Old Navy* (Annapolis: Naval Institute Press, 2002), Craig

Symonds, *Confederate Admiral: The Life and Wars of Franklin Buchanan* (Annapolis: Naval Institute Press, 1999), Gene A. Smith,
Thomas ap Catesby Jones: Commodore of Manifest Destiny (Annapolis: Naval Institute Press, 2000), and Ira Dye, *Uriah Levy, Reform-
er of the Antebellum Navy* (Gainesville: University Press of Florida,
2006). Note that the navy continued other traditional activities,
such as taking American diplomats to their posts or assisting the
army when called upon (for example, in Florida to fight Seminole
Indians): George E. Buker, *Swamp Sailors in the Second Seminole
War* (Gainesville: University Press of Florida, 2006) and R. Blake
Dunnavent, *Brown Water Warfare: The U.S. Navy in Riverine Warfare and the Emergence of a Tactical Doctrine, 1775–1970* (Gainesville: University Press of Florida, 2003), 32–44.

21. Schroeder, *Perry*, 44; Long, *Sailor-Diplomat*, 93–99, 108–11,
126–27, 131–38, 283; Richard Wheeler, *In Pirate Waters* (New York:
W. Crowell, 1969); Edward Baxter Billingsley, *In Defense of Neutral
Rights: The United States Navy and the Wars of Independence in Chile
and Peru* (Chapel Hill: University of North Carolina Press, 1967).

22. Schroeder, *Perry*, 22–23, 33–35, 97–121; Tucker, *Foote*, 35–57;
Donald L. Canney, *Africa Squadron: The U.S. Navy and the Slave
Trade, 1842–1861* (Washington DC: Potomac Books, 2008). British efforts were more serious: Ken Bourne, *Royal Navy versus the
Slave Traders: Enforcing Abolition at Sea, 1806–1898* (Barnsley: Pen
and Sword Maritime, 2007); Mark C. Hunter, *Policing the Seas: Anglo-American Relations and the Equatorial Atlantic, 1819–1865* (St.
John's, Newfoundland: International Maritime Economic History Association, 2008). In 1862 the United States, now with a government opposed to slavery, finally signed a treaty permitting each
nation to visit each other's merchant ships off Cuba and Africa.
Conway W. Henderson, "The Anglo-American Treaty of 1862 in
Civil War Diplomacy," *Civil War History* 15 (1969): 308–19; A. Taylor Milne, "The Lyons-Seward Treaty of 1862," *American Historical Review* 38 (1932–33): 511–25.

23. Steven J. Dick, *Sky and Ocean Joined: The U.S. Naval Observatory, 1830–2000* (Cambridge: Cambridge University Press, 2003), 28–38; Nathaniel Philbrick, *Sea of Glory: America's Voyage of Discovery, the U.S. Exploring Expedition, 1838–1842* (New York: Viking Penguin, 2003). For other overseas exploration such as the North Pacific Exploring Expedition, see Schroeder, *Shaping a Maritime Empire*, 159–64; A. Hunter Dupree, *Science in the Federal Government: A History of Policies and Activities to 1940* (Cambridge: Belknap Press of Harvard University Press, 1957), 95–100; and Robert Erwin Johnson, *Rear Admiral John Rodgers, 1812–1882* (Annapolis: United States Naval Institute, 1967), 101–42.

24. Belohlavek, *Foreign Policy of Jackson*, 180–92; Craig Evan Klafter, "United States Involvement in the Falkland Islands Crisis of 1831–33," *Journal of the Early Republic* 4 (1984): 395–420.

25. Smith, *Jones*, 101–24.

26. Belohlavek, *Foreign Policy of Jackson*, 151–62. For another instance of retaliation against towns in Sumatra, see Tucker, *Foote*, 27–28.

27. Schroeder, *Shaping a Maritime Empire*, 44–55, 71–73, 165–85. In 1856 the navy bombarded Chinese forts near Canton: Tucker, *Foote*, 83–96; Robert Erwin Johnson, *Far China Station: The U.S. Navy in Asian Waters, 1800–1898* (Annapolis: Naval Institute Press, 1979), 80–91; Curtis T. Henson Jr., *Commissioners and Commodores: The East India Squadron and American Diplomacy in China* (University: University of Alabama Press, 1982), 128–36.

28. Schroeder, *Rodgers*, 153–54, 165–72, and *Perry*, 48–49. Harsh discipline existed before 1815, of course; for a sophisticated explanation of its rationale, see McKee, *Gentlemanly and Honorable Profession*, 255–67. Rodgers was a disciple of his former captain, Thomas Truxtun; although strict, each did take great care to educate his junior officers.

29. Maloney, *Captain from Connecticut*, 74, 407–408; Ellis, *Mad Jack Percival*, 133–38; Ari Hoogenboom, *Gustavus Vasa Fox of*

the Union Navy: A Biography (Baltimore: Johns Hopkins University Press, 2008), 4–7, 10–24. For officers' careers, see McKee's incomparable *Gentlemanly and Honorable Profession* and Donald Chisholm, *Waiting for Dead Men's Shoes: Origins and Development of the U.S. Navy's Personnel System, 1793–1941* (Stanford: Stanford University Press, 2001), 51–219. McKee, *Gentlemanly and Honorable Profession*, 271–308, describes the system of promotion by merit prior to the War of 1812.

30. Ellis, *Mad Jack Percival*, 182–83.

31. McKee, *Gentlemanly and Honorable Profession*, 45–53; Bartlett, *Great Britain and Sea Power*, 311–13; Ellis, *Mad Jack Percival*, 141, 180. The use of alcohol aboard ship was abolished in 1862, although the Confederate navy did not follow suit: Harold D. Langley, *Social Reform in the United States Navy, 1798–1862* (Urbana: University of Illinois Press, 1967), 242–69; Harold D. Langley, "Shipboard Life," in William N. Still Jr., ed., *The Confederate Navy: The Ships, Men, and Organization, 1861–65* (London: Conway Maritime Press, 1997), 184.

32. Herman Melville, *White-Jacket, or The World in a Man-of-War* (Evanston and Chicago: Northwestern University Press and the Newberry Library, 1970) is a modern scholarly edition. For historical accounts of the sailor's lot and the abolition of flogging, see McKee, *Gentlemanly and Honorable Profession*, 219–67; Langley, *Social Reform*; Fowler, *Jack Tars and Commodores*, 126–40; Dye, *Levy*, 168–74, 181–87, 190, 198–206; W. Jeffrey Bolster, *Black Jacks: African American Seamen in the Age of Sail* (Cambridge: Harvard University Press, 1997), 223–24; Myra C. Glenn, *Campaigns against Corporal Punishment: Prisoners, Sailors, Women, and Children in Antebellum America* (Albany: State University of New York Press, 1984), 85–101, 112–21, 128–32, 155–64; James E. Valle, *Rocks & Shoals: Naval Discipline in the Age of Fighting Sail* (Annapolis: Naval Institute Press, 1980); and Jane Litten, "Navy Flogging: Captain Samuel Francis Du Pont and Tradition," *American*

Neptune 58 (1998): 145–63. Disciplinary problems continued after the abolition of flogging; see the account of an 1854–59 cruise in Lorraine McConaghy, *Warship under Sail: The USS Decatur in the Pacific West* (Seattle: University of Washington Press, 2009). For life aboard British and French ships, see Dull, *Age of the Ship of the Line*, 17–19, and Michael Lewis, *The Navy in Transition, 1814–1864: A Social History* (London: Hodder and Stoughton, 1965).

33. Schroeder, *Shaping a Maritime Empire*, 57–78; Hall, *Upshur*, 120–93, 209–13; Paolo E. Coletta, "Abel Parker Upshur," in Coletta, *American Secretaries of the Navy*, 1:176–97.

34. Silverstone, *Sailing Navy*, 36–37, 43, 49–50, 73–76; Canney, *Sailing Warships*, 71–76, 185–88; K. Jack Bauer, *Surfboats and Horse Marines: U.S. Naval Operations in the Mexican War, 1846–48* (Annapolis: United States Naval Institute, 1969), 253–59; James Phinney Baxter III, *The Introduction of the Ironclad Warship* (Cambridge: Harvard University Press, 1933; Hamden, Conn: Archon Books, 1968), 13–14. The *Michigan* was used on Lake Erie; a second iron ship, the armored "Stevens battery," ordered in 1843, was cancelled in 1862 while still incomplete: Baxter, *Introduction of the Ironclad Warship*, 41–42, 48–52, 211–19.

35. Schroeder, *Shaping a Maritime Empire*, 61–64; Bartlett, *Great Britain and Sea Power*, 9–10; Dull, *Age of the Ship of the Line*, 15; Symonds, *Confederate Admiral*, 67–82; John Niven, *Gideon Welles: Lincoln's Secretary of the Navy* (New York: Oxford University Press, 1973), 3–5, 209–17, 233; Edward P. Crapol, *John Tyler, the Accidental President* (Chapel Hill: University of North Carolina Press, 2006), 75–80; William P. Leeman, *The Long Road to Annapolis: The Founding of the Naval Academy and the Emerging American Republic* (Chapel Hill: University of North Carolina Press, 2010); Charles Todorich, *The Spirited Years: A History of the Antebellum Naval Academy* (Annapolis: Naval Institute Press, 1984); David F. Long, "The Navy under the Board of Naval Commissioners, 1815–1842" and Geoffrey S. Smith, "An Unclear Passage: The Bureaus

Run the Navy, 1842–1861," in *In Peace and War: Interpretations of American Naval History, 1775–1978*, ed. Kenneth J. Hagan (Westport CT: Greenwood Press, 1978), 63–78, 79–106.

36. David M. Pletcher, *The Diplomacy of Annexation: Texas, Oregon, and the Mexican War* (Columbia: University of Missouri Press, 1973), 197. Although many American volunteers fought in the 1836 revolt against Mexico, the U.S. government used the navy to enforce its neutrality: K. Jack Bauer, "The United States and Texas Independence: A Study in Jacksonian Integrity," *Military Affairs* 34 (1970): 44–48. Texas had its own navy: Jim Dan Hill, *The Texas Navy in Forgotten Battles and Shirtsleeve Diplomacy* (Chicago: University of Chicago Press, 1937); Tom Henderson Welles, *Commodore Moore and the Texas Navy* (Austin: University of Texas Press, 1960).

37. Pletcher, *Diplomacy of Annexation*, 260, 264, 342–43.

38. Bartlett, *Great Britain and Sea Power*, 174–76; Bourne, *Britain and the Balance of Power*, 154–58.

39. Matzke, *Deterrence through Strength*, 84–103; Pletcher, *Diplomacy of Annexation*, 402–14; Jones and Rakestraw, *Prologue to Manifest Destiny*, 151–264. For British-American relations, see also Merk, *Oregon Question* and David Dykstra, *The Shifting Balance of Power: American-British Diplomacy in North America, 1842–1848* (Oxford: University Press of America, 1999). Thomas M. Leonard, *James K. Polk: A Clear and Unquestionable Destiny* (Wilmington DE: Scholarly Resources, 2001) is a good introductory survey of Polk's diplomacy.

40. Bauer, *Surfboats and Horse Marines*, 21–22, 261–62; Baxter, *Introduction of the Ironclad Warship*, 34–35.

41. For the naval side of the war, see Bauer, *Surfboats and Horse Marines*, Schroeder, *Perry*, 127–53, Long, *Sailor-Diplomat*, 226–34, and Samuel Eliot Morison, *"Old Bruin": Commodore Matthew C. Perry, 1794–1858* (Boston: Little, Brown, 1967), 179–251. K. Jack Bauer, *The Mexican War, 1846–1848* (New York: Macmillan;

London: Collier-Macmillan, 1974), John S. D. Eisenhower, *So Far from God: The U.S. War with Mexico, 1846–1848* (New York: Random House, 1989), and David A. Clary, *Eagle and Empire: The United States, Mexico, and the Struggle for a Continent* (New York: Bantam Books, 2009) are readable histories of the war in general. For the occupation of California, see Neal Harlow, *California Conquered: War and Peace on the Pacific, 1846–1850* (Berkeley: University of California Press, 1982).

42. Andrew Lambert, *Battleships in Transition: The Creation of the Steam Battlefleet, 1815–1860* (London: Conway Maritime Press, 1994), 121–43; Roger Chesneau and Eugene M. Kolesnik, eds., *Conway's All the World's Fighting Ships, 1860–1905* (London: Conway Maritime Press, 1979), 3, 284–85. This is the first volume of a lavishly illustrated and very informative four-volume series.

43. See McConaghy, *Warship under Sail*, 175–226, 262–66, and Robert E. May, *Manifest Destiny's Underworld: Filibustering in Antebellum America* (Chapel Hill: University of North Carolina Press, 2002).

44. Schroeder, *Shaping a Maritime Empire*, 117–38; Sprout and Sprout, *Rise of American Naval Power*, 139–50; Silverstone, *Sailing Navy*, 37; Kurt Hackemer, *The U.S. Navy and the Origin of the Military Industrial Complex, 1847–1883* (Annapolis: Naval Institute Press, 2001), 28–66; Robert J. Schneller Jr., *A Quest for Glory: A Biography of Rear Admiral John A. Dahlgren* (Annapolis: Naval Institute Press, 1996), 114–25; Paul H. Silverstone, *Civil War Navies, 1855–1883* (Annapolis: Naval Institute Press, 2001), 15–18, 20–25. Silverstone also compiled *Warships of the Civil War Navies* (Annapolis: Naval Institute Press, 1989).

45. Chesneau and Kolesnik, *All the World's Fighting Ships*, 7, 116–18, 286–87; Morriss, *Cockburn*, 253–56; Bartlett, *Great Britain and Sea Power*, 216–19; Silverstone, *Civil War Navies*, 10, 14; Bauer and Roberts, *Register of Ships*, 39; Baxter, *Introduction of the Ironclad Warship*, 36–38, 48–180; Donald L. Canney, *The Old*

Steam Navy (2 vols., Annapolis: Naval Institute Press, 1990–93), 2:3–6, 12–14.

46. For the controversial Naval Efficiency Board of 1855 that purged 200 of the navy's 700 officers only to see a third of them reinstated, see Chisholm, *Waiting for Dead Men's Shoes*, 220–66, and Kevin J. Weddle, *Lincoln's Tragic Admiral: The Life of Samuel Francis Du Pont* (Charlottesville: University of Virginia Press, 2005), 59–84.

47. During one or both of Perry's two visits to Japan, his squadron contained the intimidating steam paddle frigates *Mississippi*, *Susquehanna*, and *Powhatan*. For his visits, see Schroeder, *Perry*, 154–248; Symonds, *Confederate Admiral*, 99–114; Morison, *"Old Bruin"*, 270–410; and Peter Booth Wiley, *Yankees in the Land of the Gods: Commodore Perry and the Opening of Japan* (New York: Viking, 1990).

SIX. THE CIVIL WAR

1. Silverstone, *Civil War Navies*, 13–46, 95–110; Still, ed., *Confederate Navy*, 239–44; Canney, *Lincoln's Navy*, 17; *Official Records of the Union and Confederate Navies in the War of the Rebellion* (31 vols., Washington DC: Government Printing Office, 1894–1927), ser. 1, 1:xv–xvi; William S. Dudley, *Going South: U.S. Navy Officer Resignations and Dismissals on the Eve of the Civil War* (Washington DC: Naval Historical Foundation, 1981); Mark C. Hunter, *A Society of Gentlemen: Midshipmen at the U.S. Naval Academy, 1845–1861* (Annapolis: Naval Institute Press, 2010), 151–54; Craig L. Symonds, *Lincoln and His Admirals: Abraham Lincoln, the U.S. Navy, and the Civil War* (Oxford: Oxford University Press, 2008), 54; James M. McPherson, *Battle Cry of Freedom: The Civil War Era* (Oxford: Oxford University Press, 1988), 313. McPherson's magnificent book is a superb introduction to the war. For a different perspective, see Mark A. Neely Jr., *The Civil War and the Limits of Destruction* (Cambridge: Harvard University Press, 2007). Craig Symonds is the dean of American naval historians; see also his

Civil War at Sea (Santa Barbara: ABC-CLIO, 2009). Recent general surveys of the naval history of the war include William H. Roberts, *Now for the Contest: Coastal and Oceanic Naval Operations in the Civil War* (Lincoln: University of Nebraska Press, 2004); Spencer C. Tucker, *A Short History of the Civil War at Sea* (Wilmington DE: Scholarly Resources, 2002) and *Blue and Gray Navies: The Civil War Afloat* (Annapolis: Naval Institute Press, 2006); William M. Fowler Jr., *Under Two Flags: The American Navy in the Civil War* (New York: W. W. Norton, 1990); and Ivan Musicant, *Divided Waters: The Naval History of the Civil War* (New York: HarperCollins, 1995). Spencer C. Tucker, *The Civil War Naval Encyclopedia* (2 vols., Santa Barbara: ABC-CLIO, 2011), and Donald Stoker, *The Grand Design: Strategy and the American Civil War* (Oxford: Oxford University Press, 2010) are useful.

2. Symonds, *Lincoln and His Admirals*, 131–32; Hoogenboom, *Fox*, 186–87; Tucker, *Foote*, 82–83, and *Arming the Fleet*, 200–216, 233–36; Chesneau and Kolesnik, *All the World's Fighting Ships*, 112; Schneller, *Quest for Glory*, 73–175. David G. Surdam, "The Union Navy's Blockade Reconsidered," in *Naval Blockades and Seapower: Strategies and Counter-Strategies, 1805–2005*, ed. Bruce A. Eileman and S. C. M. Paine (London: Routledge, 2006), 63, compares the 1860 manufacturing production of the future Confederate states with the United States as a whole.

3. Chisholm, *Waiting for Dead Men's Shoes*, 271–315. For Welles, see also Niven, *Welles,* and Howard K. Beale and Alan S. Broadsword, eds., *Diary of Gideon Welles, Secretary of the Navy under Lincoln and Johnson* (3 vols., New York: W. W. Norton, 1960).

4. Tucker, *Foote*; Lewis, *Farragut*; Robert J. Schneller Jr., *Farragut: America's First Admiral* (Washington: Brassey's, 2002); Chester G. Hearn, *Admiral David Dixon Porter: The Civil War Years* (Annapolis: Naval Institute Press, 1996) and *Admiral David Glasgow Farragut: The Civil War Years* (Annapolis: Naval Institute Press, 1998).

5. Symonds, *Lincoln and His Admirals*, 3–36; Niven, *Welles,*

324–39; Hoogenboom, *Fox*, 57–71; Hearn, *Porter*, 36–52; Russell McClintock, *Lincoln and the Decision for War: The Northern Response to Secession* (Chapel Hill: University of North Carolina Press, 2008); David Detzer, *Allegiance: Fort Sumter, Charleston, and the Beginning of the Civil War* (New York: Harcourt, 2001); Maury Klein, *Days of Defiance: Sumter, Secession, and the Coming of the Civil War* (New York: Alfred A. Knopf, 1997); Adam Goodheart, *1861: The Civil War Awakening* (New York: Alfred A. Knopf, 2011), 134–84. For the three warships, see Silverstone, *Civil War Navies*, 14, 25, 45, 138.

6. Robert M. Browning, "The Confederate States Navy Department," in *Confederate Navy*, ed. Still, 31; Symonds, *Confederate Admiral*, 146–51. Raimondo Luraghi, *A History of the Confederate Navy* (Annapolis: Naval Institute Press, 1996) provides a lengthy general history of Confederate naval operations, but it is not always reliable because of the author's extreme partiality for the Confederacy.

7. Symonds, *Civil War at Sea*, 63–65.

8. The classic study is Frank Lawrence Owlsley, *King Cotton Diplomacy: Foreign Relations of the Confederate States of America* (2nd ed., Chicago: University of Chicago Press, 1931), although it must be used with caution because of its extreme pro-Confederate bias. A recent analysis, moreover, disputes Owlsley's assertion that the supply of cotton in Britain at the beginning of the war was unusually high: David G. Surdam, *Northern Naval Supremacy and the Economics of the American Civil War* (Columbia: University of South Carolina Press, 2001), 125–29, 148; see also Davis and Engerman, *Naval Blockades in Peace and War*, 143–49. Other studies of Civil War diplomacy include Howard Jones, *Union in Peril: The Crisis over British Intervention in the Civil War* (Chapel Hill: University of North Carolina Press, 1992), *Lincoln and a New Birth of Freedom: The Union and Slavery in the Diplomacy of the Civil War* (Lincoln: University of Nebraska Press, 1997), and

Blue & Gray Diplomacy: A History of Union and Confederate Foreign Relations (Lexington: University of Kentucky Press, 2010); Lynn Case and Warren F. Spencer, *The United States and France: Civil War Diplomacy* (Philadelphia: University of Pennsylvania Press, 1970); David Paul Crook, *The North, the South, and the Great Powers* (New York: Wiley, 1974); Dean B. Mahin, *One War at a Time: The International Dimensions of the American Civil War* (Washington DC: Brassey's, 1999); Brian Jenkins, *Britain and the War for the Union* (2 vols., Montreal: McGill-Queens University Press, 1974–80); Philip E. Myers, *Caution and Cooperation: The Civil War in British-American Relations* (Kent OH: Kent State University Press, 2008); Charles M. Hubbard, *The Burden of Southern Diplomacy* (Knoxville: University of Tennessee Press, 1998); and Amanda Foreman, *A World on Fire: Britain's Crucial Role in the American Civil War* (New York: Random House, 2010).

9. Jones, *Union in Peril*, 80–99, and *Blue & Gray Diplomacy*, 83–113; Symonds, *Lincoln and His Admirals*, 71–97; Norman B. Ferris, *Desperate Diplomacy: William H. Seward's Foreign Policy, 1861* (Knoxville: University of Tennessee Press, 1976) and *The Trent Affair: A Diplomatic Crisis* (Knoxville: University of Tennessee Press, 1977); Kenneth Bourne, "British Preparations for War with the North, 1861–1862," *English Historical Review* 76 (1961): 600–632, and *Britain and the Balance of Power*, 211–47; Regis A. Courtemache, *No Need of Glory: The British Navy in American Waters, 1860–64* (Annapolis: Naval Institute Press, 1977), 39–65. Part of the British willingness to accept an American apology was their fear of a European crisis occurring while they were at war with the United States. This fear was later reinforced by the Russian suppression of a revolt in Poland in 1863. During that year the Russians sent fleets to New York and San Francisco, which Americans viewed as support for the Union cause: Herring, *From Colony to Superpower*, 245–46; Albert A. Woldman, *Lincoln and the Russians* (Westport CT: Greenwood, 1952), 140–55; Norman

E. Saul, *Distant Friends: The United States and Russia, 1763–1867* (Lawrence: University of Kansas Press, 1991), 339–54. Conversely the British feared an American attack on Canada if they should become involved in a naval war in Europe: Hamilton, *Anglo-French Naval Rivalry*, 305.

10. Hoogenboom, *Fox*, 82–88; Symonds, *Civil War at Sea*, 34–35; Silverstone, *Civil War Navies*, 30–33, 47–78; Weddle, *Lincoln's Tragic Admiral*, 106–24; Edward William Sloan III, *Benjamin Franklin Isherwood, Naval Engineer: The Years as Engineer in Chief, 1861–1869* (Annapolis: United States Naval Institute, 1965), 30–33.

11. The best account of these operations is in the indispensable book by Rowena Reed, *Combined Operations in the Civil War* (Annapolis: Naval Institute Press, 1978), 3–63. See also Weddle, *Lincoln's Tragic Admiral*, 125–53; Johnson, *Rodgers*, 172–80; John D. Hayes, ed., *Samuel Francis Du Pont: A Selection from His Civil War Letters* (3 vols., Ithaca NY: Cornell University Press, 1969), 1:123–425; and Robert M. Browning Jr., *Success Is All That Was Expected: The South Atlantic Blockading Squadron during the Civil War* (Washington DC: Brassey's, 2002), 23–95. Other books on joint operations include David Page, *Ship versus Shore: Civil War Engagements along Southern Shores and Rivers* (Nashville: Rutledge Hall Press, 1994); Charles Dana Gibson, *Assault and Logistics* (2 vols., Camden ME: Ensign Press, 1995); and Craig L. Symonds, ed., *Union Coastal Operations in the Civil War* (New York: Fordham University Press, 2010).

12. See Joseph T. Durkin, *Stephen Mallory: Confederate Navy Chief* (Chapel Hill: University of North Carolina Press, 1954). Koistinen, *Beating Plowshares into Swords*, 258–64, provides a perceptive critique of Mallory's administration of the navy.

13. Warren F. Spencer, *The Confederate Navy in Europe* (Tuscaloosa: University of Alabama Press, 1983), 67; Davis and Engerman, *Naval Blockades in Peace and War*, 130. For the cruisers, see Symonds, *Civil War at Sea*, 59–85; Chester G. Hearn, *Gray Raiders*

of the Sea: How Eight Confederate Warships Destroyed the Union's High Seas Commerce (Camden ME: International Marine, 1992); James Tertius de Kay, *The Rebel Raiders: The Astonishing History of the Confederacy's Secret Navy* (New York: Ballantine, 2002); Coy F. Cross II, *Lincoln's Man in Liverpool: Consul Dudley and the Legal Battle to Stop Confederate Warships* (DeKalb: Northern Illinois University Press, 2007); Richard I. Lester, *Confederate Finance and Purchasing in Great Britain* (Charlottesville: University Press of Virginia, 1975), 61–133; Frank J. Merli, *Great Britain and the Confederate Navy, 1861–1865* (Bloomington: Indiana University Press, 1970) and *The* Alabama, *British Neutrality, and the American Civil War* (Bloomington: Indiana University Press, 2004); Charles Grayson Summersell, css Alabama: *Builder, Captain, and Plans* (University: University of Alabama Press, 1985); Charles M. Robinson III, *Shark of the Confederacy: The Story of the css* Alabama (Annapolis: Naval Institute Press, 1995); Stephen Fox, *Wolf of the Deep: Raphael Semmes and the Notorious Confederate Raider css* Alabama (New York: Alfred A. Knopf, 2007); Warren F. Spencer, *Raphael Semmes: The Philosophical Mariner* (Tuscaloosa: University of Alabama Press, 1957); William Marvel, *The* Alabama & *the* Kearsarge: *The Sailor's Civil War* (Chapel Hill: University of North Carolina Press, 1996); John M. Taylor, *Confederate Raider: Raphael Semmes of the* Alabama (New York: Brassey's, 1994); Frank L. Owlsley Jr., *The* css Florida: *Her Building and Operations* (Philadelphia: University of Pennsylvania Press, 1965); Roger G. Shingleton, *High Seas Confederate: The Life and Times of John Newland Moffitt* (Columbia: University of South Carolina Press, 1994); and Tom Chaffin, *Sea of Gray: The Around-the-World Odyssey of the Confederate Raider* Shenandoah (New York: Hill and Wang, 2006).

14. Johnson, *Rodgers*, 151–55; Sloan, *Isherwood*, 21–26; Jay Slagle, *Ironclad Captain: Seth Ledyard Phelps and the U.S. Navy, 1841–1864* (Kent OH: Kent State University Press, 1996), 1–7; Maurice Melton, "Facilities," in *Confederate Navy*, ed. Still, 70–72; Canney,

Lincoln's Navy, 17; Field, *Confederate Ironclad vs. Union Ironclad,* 10–12; Carl D. Park, *Ironclad Down: The uss Merrimack–css Virginia: From Construction to Destruction* (Annapolis: Naval Institute Press, 2007); John V. Quarstein, "Sink before Surrender: The Story of the css Virginia," in *The Battle of Hampton Roads: New Perspectives on the uss Monitor and css Virginia,* ed. Harold Holzer and Tim Mulligan (New York: Fordham University Press, 2006), 57–63. The fabled frigate *United States* also was spared from the fire and was later used as a receiving ship under the name *Confederate States:* Johnson, *Rodgers,* 153; Silverstone, *Civil War Navies,* 186.

15. Reed, *Combined Operations,* 3–7; Canney, *Old Steam Navy,* 2:38–55; Tucker, *Foote,* 116–22; Silverstone, *Civil War Navies,* 114–17, 168–84; Slagle, *Ironclad Captain,* 112–50; Johnson, *Rodgers,* 156–68; Gary D. Joiner, *Mr. Lincoln's Brown Water Navy: The Mississippi Squadron* (Lanham MD: Rowman and Littlefield, 2007), 13–31; Florence L. Dorsey, *Road to the Sea: The Story of James P. Eads and the Mississippi River* (New York: Rinehart, 1947), 59–66; Myron J. Smith, *The Timberclads in the Civil War: The Lexington, Conestoga, and Tyler on the Western Waters* (Jefferson NC: McFarland, 2008), *Tinclads in the Civil War: Union Light-Draught Combat Operations in Western Waters, 1862–1865* (Jefferson NC: McFarland, 2010), and *The uss Carondelet: A Civil War Ironclad on Western Waters* (Jefferson NC: McFarland, 2010); Edwin C. Bearss, *Hardluck Ironclad: The Sinking and Salvage of the Cairo* (Baton Rouge: Louisiana State University Press, 1966); Elizabeth Hoxie Joyner, *The uss Cairo: History and Artifacts of a Civil War Gunboat* (Jefferson NC: McFarland, 2006); Angus Konstam, *Union River Ironclad, 1861–1865* (Long Island City NY: Osprey, 2002) and *Mississippi River Gunboats of the American Civil War, 1861–65* (Long Island City NY: Osprey, 2002), 4–8, 12–16; Larry J. Daniel and Lynn N. Bock, *Island No. 10: Struggle for the Mississippi Valley* (Tuscaloosa: University of Alabama Press, 1996), 11–14, 101–103.

16. Smith, *Timberclads,* 146–65; Nathaniel Chearis Hughes Jr.,

The Battle of Belmont: Grant Strikes South (Chapel Hill: University of North Carolina Press, 1996); Bruce Catton, *Grant Moves South* (Boston: Little, Brown, 1960), 74–84.

17. Slagle, *Ironclad Captain*, 143–73; Smith, *Timberclads*, 189–224; Reed, *Combined Operations*, 76–87; Tucker, *Foote*, 136–47; Catton, *Grant Moves South*, 125–26, 130–45; Benjamin Franklin Cooling, *Forts Henry and Donelson: The Key to the Confederate Heartland* (Knoxville: University of Tennessee Press, 1987), 1–121; Jack Hurst, *Men of Fire: Grant, Forrest, and the Campaign That Decided the Civil War* (New York: Basic Books, 2007); Spencer C. Tucker, *Unconditional Surrender: The Capture of Forts Henry and Donelson* (Abilene: McWhitney Foundation Press, 2001), 13–60. Thomas Lawrence Connelly's *Army of the Heartland: The Army of Tennessee, 1861–1862* (Baton Rouge: Louisiana State University Press, 1967) is a superb study of Confederate strategy during the campaign.

18. Slagle, *Ironclad Captain*, 174–88; Catton, *Grant Moves South*, 145–78; Cooling, *Forts Henry and Donelson*, 122–244; Tucker, *Unconditional Surrender*, 61–116; Stephen D. Engle, *Struggle for the Heartland: The Campaigns from Fort Henry to Corinth* (Lincoln: University of Nebraska Press, 2001), 63–93.

19. Smith, *Timberclads*, 272–311; Slagle, *Ironclad Captain*, 189–208; Tucker, *Foote*, 163–87; Catton, *Grant Moves South*, 216–64; Daniel and Bock, *Island No. 10*; James Lee McDonough, *Shiloh—In Hell before Night* (Knoxville: University of Tennessee Press, 1977); Wiley Sword, *Shiloh: Bloody April* (New York: William Morrow, 1974); Larry J. Daniel, *Shiloh: The Battle That Changed the Civil War* (New York: Simon & Schuster, 1997). There is an excellent map of Island No. 10 and the surrounding defenses in John C. Wideman, *Civil War Chronicles: Naval Warfare, Courage, and Combat on the Water* (New York: MetroBooks, 1997), 57.

20. For the use of mortar ships in the Crimean War, see Hamilton, *Anglo-French Naval Rivalry*, 77–78, 126; D. K. Brown, *Before*

the *Ironclad: Development of Ship Design, Propulsion, and Armament in the Royal Navy, 1815–60* (London: Conway Maritime Press, 1990), 154–56; and Andrew D. Lambert, *The Crimean War: British Grand Strategy, 1853–1856* (Manchester: Manchester University Press, 1990), 256–60, 281–95. For Porter's visiting one, see Hearn, *Porter*, 33. For Farragut's selection and his subsequent naval operations on the Mississippi, see Lewis, *Farragut*, 2:2–134; Schneller, *Farragut*, 29–77; Hoogenboom, *Fox*, 140–51; Chester G. Hearn, *The Capture of New Orleans, 1862* (Baton Rouge: Louisiana State University Press, 1995), *Porter*, 68–138, and *Farragut*, 41–220; Dudley Taylor Cornish and Virginia Jeans Laas, *Lincoln's Lee: The Life of Samuel Phillips Lee, United States Navy, 1812–1897* (Lawrence: University Press of Kansas, 1986), 1–4, 95–107; and Robert Underwood Johnson and Clarence Clough Buel, eds., *Battles and Leaders of the Civil War, Being for the Most Part Contributions by Union and Confederate Officers* (4 vols., New York: Century, 1887–88), 2:13–102.

21. For the first two, see Robert J. Browning Jr., *From Cape Charles to Cape Fear: The North Atlantic Blockading Squadron during the Civil War* (Tuscaloosa: University of Alabama Press, 1993) and *Success Is All That Was Expected*. Stephen R. Taafe, *Commanding Lincoln's Navy: Union Naval Leadership during the Civil War* (Annapolis: Naval Institute Press, 2009) appraises the commanders of the four blockading squadrons as well as the commanders of the West India squadron and the Mississippi squadron.

22. For the opposing naval forces, see Silverstone, *Civil War Navies*, 13–14, 20–23, 31–33, 62, 98, 152–53; William N. Still, *Iron Afloat: The Story of the Confederate Armorclads* (Nashville: Vanderbilt University Press, 1971), 41–61; and Maurice Melton, "Shipbuilding," in *Confederate Navy*, ed. Still, 96–99. For Mallory's withholding gunboats, see Durkin, *Mallory*, 203–208, 245–46.

23. Lewis, *Farragut*, 2:78–123; Schneller, *Farragut*, 53–59; Reed, *Combined Operations*, 195–202; Slagle, *Ironclad Captain*, 210–40,

249–59; Chester G. Hearn, *Ellet's Brigade: The Strangest Outfit of All* (Baton Rouge: Louisiana State University Press, 2000), 27–60; and *Porter*, 119–34.

24. Smith, *Timberclads*, 344–60, 367–93, and *Tinclads*, 88–90, 94, 100–103; Slagle, *Ironclad Captain*, 258–80; Still, *Iron Afloat*, 62–78; Hearn, *Porter*, 141–74; R. Thomas Campbell, *Sea Hawk of the Confederacy: Lt. Charles W. Read and the Confederate Navy* (Shippensburg PA: Burd Street Press, 2000); Larry J. Daniel, *Days of Glory: The Army of the Cumberland, 1861–1865* (Baton Rouge: Louisiana State University Press, 2004), 184, 198–225.

25. Silverstone, *Civil War Navies*, 114–15, 152; Still, *Iron Afloat*, 8–40; Roberts, *Now for the Contest*, 81, 89; Quarstein, "Sink before Surrender," and Craig L. Symonds, "Building the Ironclads," in *Battle of Hampton Roads*, ed. Holzer and Mulligan, 23–26, 57–83; Field, *Confederate Ironclad vs. Union Ironclad*, 10–18, 29; George M. Brooke Jr., *John M. Brooke, Naval Scientist and Educator* (Charlottesville: University Press of Virginia, 1980), 231–51.

26. Baxter, *Introduction of the Ironclad Warship*, 245–69; Canney, *Old Steam Navy*, 2:15–34; Symonds, *Lincoln and His Admirals*, 131–36; Hoogenboom, *Fox*, 107–11; Silverstone, *Civil War Navies*, 4, 11; Field, *Confederate Ironclad vs. Union Ironclad*, 18–31; Symonds, "Building the Ironclads" and David Mindell, "Iron Horse, Iron Coffin: Life aboard the USS *Monitor*" in *Battle of Hampton Roads*, ed. Holzer and Mulligan, 26–34, 37–55; Johnson, *Rodgers*, 223–24; David A. Mindell, *War, Technology and Experience aboard the USS Monitor* (Baltimore: Johns Hopkins University Press, 2000). For the career of the *New Ironsides*, see William H. Roberts, *USS New Ironsides in the Civil War* (Annapolis: Naval Institute Press, 1999). For a comparison of European ironclads to it, see Chesneau and Kolesnik, *All the World's Fighting Ships*, 7–11, 118, 286–87. Chief Engineer Benjamin Franklin Isherwood wished to build more ironclads like it for potential use as commerce raiders against European enemies, but Welles rebuffed him: Sloan, *Isherwood*, 52–65.

27. The British navy also was experimenting with turrets, and on 29 April 1862 it laid down its first turret ship, the *Royal Albert*. The Confederates used the British turret design for two ships it constructed in an English shipyard, the so-called Laird rams. After their launching, the British then purchased the ships for their own navy in order to preserve British neutrality: Baxter, *Introduction of the Ironclad Warship*, 181–95; Chesneau and Kolesnik, *All the World's Fighting Ships*, 4–5, 19–20; Spencer, *Confederate Navy in Europe*, 66, 83, 104–15.

28. Holzer and Mulligan, eds., *Battle of Hampton Roads*; Field, *Confederate Ironclad vs. Union Ironclad*, 40–60; Symonds, *Confederate Admiral*, 156–71, and *Decision at Sea*, 83–137; Silverstone, *Civil War Navies*, 16–17, 95, 97; Gene A. Smith, *Iron and Heavy Guns: Duel between the Monitor and Merrimac* (Abilene: McWhitney Foundation Press, 1998); William C. Davis, *Duel between the First Ironclads* (Baton Rouge: Louisiana State University Press, 1975).

29. Reed, *Combined Operations*, 121–60; Symonds, *Lincoln and His Admirals*, 145–56.

30. Canney, *Old Steam Navy*, 2:57–93; Silverstone, *Civil War Navies*, 3–10, 111–14, 152–57; Still, *Iron Afloat*, 93–105; Hoogenboom, *Fox*, 285–88; Johnson, *Rodgers*, 282–97; William H. Roberts, *Civil War Ironclads: The U.S. Navy and Industrial Mobilization* (Baltimore: Johns Hopkins University Press, 2002); Howard J. Fuller, *Clad in Iron: The American Civil War and the Challenge of British Naval Power* (Westport CT: Praeger, 2008), 271–82; Roger Chesneau, ed., *Conway's All the World's Fighting Ships, 1922–1946* (London: Conway Maritime Press, 1980), 9–10, 17. In addition to the river monitors, the Union eventually converted or constructed fifteen "Pook turtles" and other river ironclads and more than seventy lightly armored "tinclads" for use on inland waters: Smith, *Tinclads*, 341–44; Silverstone, *Civil War Navies*, 111–38; Canney, *Old Steam Navy*, 2:95–118; Konstam, *Mississippi River Gunboats*, 36–40.

31. Reed, *Combined Operations*, 161–70; Mindell, *War, Technology, and Experience*, 94–103; Johnson, *Rodgers*, 194–207, 211–13; Brian K. Burton, *Extraordinary Circumstances: The Seven Days Battles* (Bloomington: Indiana University Press, 2001), 62, 345; Stephen W. Sears, *George B. McClellan: The Young Napoleon* (New York: Ticknor and Fields, 1988), 184, 188–89, 202, and *To the Gates of Richmond: The Peninsula Campaign* (New York: Ticknor and Fields, 1992), 93–94; Royce Gordon Shingleton, *John Taylor Wood, Sea Ghost of the Confederacy* (Athens: University of Georgia Press, 1979), 45–53. Lee feared that McClellan would shift to the James: Joseph L. Harsh, *Confederate Tide Rising: Robert E. Lee and the Making of Confederate Strategy, 1861–1862* (Kent OH: Kent State University Press, 1998), 66, 77, 95. For the location of Confederate facilities along the Richmond waterfront, see the map in Maurice Melton, "Facilities," in *Confederate Navy*, ed. Still, 84; for the *Naugatuck*, see Baxter, *Introduction of the Ironclad Warship*, 217, and Johnson, *Rodgers*, 200–201.

32. Jones, *Blue & Gray Diplomacy*, 181–204, and *Union in Peril*, 138–230; Owlsley, *King Cotton Diplomacy*, 134–53; Howard J. Fuller, *Clad in Iron*, 169–73, 264, 282–85, and "'This Country Now Occupies the Vantage Ground': Union Monitors vs. the British Navy," in *Battle of Hampton Roads*, ed. Holzer and Mulligan, 125–39.

33. Reed, *Combined Operations*, 263–94; Symonds, *Civil War at Sea*, 119–33; Taafe, *Commanding Lincoln's Navy*, 129–50; Niven, *Welles*, 432–39; Roberts, *USS New Ironsides in the Civil War*, 44–56; Davis and Engerman, *Naval Blockades in Peace and War*, 137–40; Weddle, *Lincoln's Tragic Admiral*, 154–207; Donald S. Frazier, *Fire in the Cane Field: The Federal Invasion of Louisiana and Texas, January 1861–January 1863* (Buffalo Gap TX: State House Press, 2009), 263–303, 311–15; Steven R. Wise, *Gate of Hell: Campaign for Charleston Harbor, 1863* (Columbia: University of South Carolina Press, 1994), 1–32.

34. Browning, *From Cape Charles to Cape Fear*, 63–67; H. J. Eckenrode and Bryan Conrad, *James Longstreet, Lee's War Horse* (Chapel Hill: University of North Carolina Press, 1936), 154–67; Stephen Sears, *Gettysburg* (Boston: Houghton Mifflin, 2003), 47–49. General P. G. T. Beauregard commanded about 20,000 troops in South Carolina, Georgia, and Florida, of which about 6,500 were in the Charleston area: Wise, *Gate of Hell*, 222–27.

35. Reed, *Combined Operations*, 243–60; Hearn, *Porter*, 177–237, and *Farragut*, 189–220; Lewis, *Farragut*, 2:165–210; Catton, *Grant Moves South*, 407–83; William L. Shea and Terence J. Winschel, *Vicksburg Is the Key: The Struggle for the Mississippi River* (Lincoln: University of Nebraska Press, 2003), 106–78; Michael B. Ballard, *Vicksburg: The Campaign That Opened the Mississippi* (Chapel Hill: University of North Carolina Press, 2004).

36. For a description, see David G. Chandler, *The Campaigns of Napoleon* (New York: Macmillan, 1966), 162–63.

37. Hearn, *Porter*, 209–39; Smith, *Timberclads*, 412–23, and *Tinclads*, 131–38; Slagle, *Ironclad Captain*, 335–36; Lewis, *Farragut*, 2:198–210; Shea and Winschel, *Vicksburg*, 187–204; John D. Milligan, *Gunboats Down the Mississippi* (Annapolis: Naval Institute Press, 1965), 143–76; Allan Keller, *Morgan's Raid* (Indianapolis: Bobbs-Merrill, 1961), 63, 101–105, 173–77, 186.

38. Reed, *Combined Operations*, 295–320; Wise, *Gate of Hell*, 33–218; Roberts, *uss New Ironsides in the Civil War*, 67–79; E. Milby Burton, *The Siege of Charleston, 1861–1865* (Columbia: University of South Carolina Press, 1970), 151–210.

39. Daniel, *Days of Glory*, 367, 372; Peter Cozzens, *The Shipwreck of Their Hopes: The Battles for Chattanooga* (Urbana: University of Illinois Press, 1994), 48–65; Bruce Catton, *Grant Takes Command* (Boston: Little, Brown, 1968), 22–85.

40. Slagle, *Ironclad Captain*, 343–81; Smith, *Timberclads*, 432–64, and *Tinclads*, 168–69, 173–77, 192–95, 202–10; Hearn, *Porter*, 243–65; Silverstone, *Civil War Navies*, 111–12, 114–15, 119,

126; William R. Brooksher, *War along the Bayous: The 1864 Red River Campaign in Louisiana* (Washington: Brassey's, 1998); H. Ludwell Johnson, *Red River Campaign: Politics and Cotton in the Civil War* (Baltimore: Johns Hopkins University Press, 1958); Gary D. Joiner, *Through the Howling Wilderness: The 1864 Red River Campaign and Union Failure in the West* (Knoxville: University of Tennessee Press, 2006).

41. Still, *Iron Afloat*, 170–86; Symonds, *Lincoln and His Admirals*, 316–21; Taafe, *Commanding Lincoln's Navy*, 237–38; Cornish and Laas, *Lincoln's Lee*, 130–35, 217–18n; Catton, *Grant Takes Command*, 255, 280–85; Benjamin Franklin Cooling, *Jubal Early's Raid on Washington, 1864* (Baltimore: Nautical and Aviation Publishing Company of America, 1989); Jeffrey D. Wert, *From Winchester to Cedar Creek: The Shenandoah Campaign of 1864* (Carlisle PA: South Mountain Press, 1987). For the effects of hunger on Lee's army over the winter of 1864–65, see J. Tracy Power, *Lee's Miserables: Life in the Army of Northern Virginia from the Wilderness to Appomattox* (Chapel Hill: University of North Carolina Press, 1998), 257–60; Joseph T. Glatthaar, *General Lee's Army: From Victory to Collapse* (New York: Free Press, 2008), 434–62; and Richard D. Goff, *Confederate Supply* (Durham: Duke University Press, 1969), 223–27, 230–33.

42. Symonds, *Confederate Admiral*, 189–219; Still, *Iron Afloat*, 187–211; Lewis, *Farragut*, 2:252–82; Hearn, *Farragut*, 235–303; Schneller, *Farragut*, 78–93; Jack Friend, *West Wind, Flood Tide: The Battle of Mobile Bay* (Annapolis: Naval Institute Press, 2004); Chester Hearn, *Mobile Bay and the Mobile Campaign: The Last Great Battles of the Civil War* (Jefferson NC: McFarland, 1993). For Maury's work on "torpedoes" and his other services to the Confederacy, see Spencer, *Confederate Navy in Europe*, 127–46; Frances Leigh Williams, *Matthew Fontaine Maury: Scientist of the Sea* (New Brunswick NJ: Rutgers University Press, 1963), 365–420; and Timothy S. Wolters, "Electric Torpedoes in the Confederacy:

Reconciling Conflicting Histories," *Journal of Military History* 72 (2008): 755–83.

43. Cornish and Laas, *Lincoln's Lee*, 142–50; Smith, *Tinclads*, 294–311; Wiley Sword, *Embrace an Angry Wind: The Confederacy's Last Hurrah: Spring Hill, Franklin, and Nashville* (New York: HarperCollins, 1992), 284–85, 326, 421; James Lee McDonough, *Nashville: The Western Confederacy's Final Gamble* (Knoxville: University of Tennessee Press, 2004), 157.

44. Cornish and Laas, *Lincoln's Lee*, 142–50; Reed, *Combined Operations*, 321–83; Hearn, *Porter*, 297–306; Roberts, *uss* New Ironsides *in the Civil War*, 95–103; Chris E. Fonvielle Jr., *Last Rays of Departing Hope: The Wilmington Campaign* (Campbell CA: Savas, 1997); Rod Gragg, *Confederate Goliath: The Battle of Fort Fisher* (Baton Rouge: Louisiana State University Press, 1994); Charles M. Robinson III, *Hurricane of Fire: The Union Assault on Fort Fisher* (Annapolis: Naval Institute Press, 1998).

45. Chaffin, *Sea of Gray*, 301.

46. Royce Shingleton, "Seamen, Landsmen, Firemen, and Coal Heavers," in *Confederate Navy*, ed. Still, 135; Roberts, *Now for the Contest*, 29, 143–44; Browning, *From Cape Charles to Cape Fear*, 200; Canney, *Lincoln's Navy*, 117–18; Michael Bennett, *Union Jacks: Yankee Sailors in the Civil War* (Chapel Hill: University of North Carolina Press, 1994); Steven J. Ramold, *Slaves, Sailors, Citizens: African Americans in the Union Navy* (DeKalb: Northern Illinois University Press, 2002); Dennis J. Ringle, *Life in Mr. Lincoln's Navy* (Annapolis: Naval Institute Press, 1998); William N. Still Jr., "The Yankee Bluejacket" and "The Confederate Tar," in William N. Still Jr., John M. Taylor, and Norman C. Delaney, *Raiders and Blockaders: The American Civil War Afloat* (Washington DC: Brassey's, 1998), 52–79, 80–99. Part of the advantage of the Union navy (like the Union army) was the service rendered by nearly 20,000 African American crewmen among the 120,000 crewmen who served during the war: Canney, *Lincoln's*

Navy, 138–39; Ringle, *Life in Mr. Lincoln's Navy*, 11–16; Bennett, *Union Jacks*, 12, 155–81; David L. Valuska, *The African American in the Union Navy, 1861–1865* (New York: Garland, 1993); Barbara Brooks Tomblin, *Bluejackets and Contrabands: African Americans and the Union Navy* (Lexington: University Press of Kentucky, 2009); Steven J. Ramold, *Slaves, Sailors, Citizens: African Americans in the Union Navy* (DeKalb: Northern Illinois University Press, 2002).

47. Slagle, *Ironclad Captain*, 234–39; Konstam, *Mississippi River Gunboats*, 14–16, 34–35, 42–44; Silverstone, *Civil War Navies*, 168–69; R. Thomas Campbell, *Confederate Naval Forces in Western Waters: The Defense of the Mississippi River and Its Tributaries* (Jefferson NC: McFarland, 2005), 94–98. Belief in the ram was widely shared, in Europe, and some French naval theoreticians advocated the use of the melee: Hamilton, *Anglo-French Naval Rivalry*, 114–17.

48. Still, *Iron Afloat*, 158–62; Browning, *From Cape Charles to Cape Fear*, 100–106. For the eventual destruction of the *Albemarle*, see Browning, 107–14; Robert C. Elliot, *Ironclad of the Roanoke: Gilbert Elliot's Albemarle* (Shippensburg PA: White Mane, 1994); and Alden R. Carter, *The Sea Eagle: The Civil War Memoir of Lt. Cdr. William B. Cushing, USN* (Latham MD: Rowman and Littlefield, 2009).

49. Browning, "Confederate States Navy Department" in *Confederate Navy*, ed. Still, 21–39; Canney, *Lincoln's Navy*, 22–32; Tom Henderson Wells, *The Confederate Navy: A Study in Organization* (University: University of Alabama Press, 1971); William N. Still Jr., *Confederate Shipbuilding* (Athens: University of Georgia Press, 1969).

50. William C. Davis, *Look Away! A History of the Confederate States of America* (New York: Free Press, 2002); Stephanie McCurry, *Confederate Reckoning: Power and Politics in the Civil War South* (Cambridge: Harvard University Press, 2010); Barrington

Moore Jr., *Social Origins of Dictatorship and Democracy: Lord and Peasant in the Making of the Modern World* (Boston: Beacon Press, 1966), 111–55; Emory M. Thomas, *The Confederate Nation, 1861–1865* (New York: Harper and Row, 1979); Susan Dunn, *Dominion of Memories: Jefferson, Madison, and the Decline of Virginia* (New York: Basic Books, 2007).

51. Fuller, *Clad in Iron*, 184; McPherson, *Battle Cry of Freedom*, 437–53; Koistinen, *Beating Plowshares into Swords*, 186, 194; Jay Sexton, *Debtor Diplomacy: Finances and Foreign Relations in the Civil War Era, 1837–1873* (Oxford: Clarendon Press, 2005), 82–189; Richard Cecil Todd, *Confederate Finance* (Athens: University of Georgia Press, 1954); Douglas M. Ball, *Financial Failure and Confederate Defeat* (Urbana: University of Illinois Press, 1991). The most rigorous analysis of the effects of the blockade is Surdam, *Northern Naval Supremacy*, but see also Koistinen, *Beating Plowshares into Swords*, 229–32, 248–52, and Davis and Engerman, *Naval Blockades in Peace and War*, 109–58. For Confederate blockade running, see also Roberts, *Now for the Contest*, 101–19; Browning, *From Cape Charles to Cape Fear*, 249–70; Goff, *Confederate Supply*, 43–47, 120–21, 144–47, 153, 175–84, 225; and Stephen R. Wise, *Lifeline of the Confederacy: Blockade Running during the Civil War* (Columbia: University of South Carolina Press, 1988).

52. John Majewski, *Modernizing a Slave Economy: The Economic Vision of the Confederate Nation* (Chapel Hill: University of North Carolina Press, 2009), 146–51; William J. Cooper, *Jefferson Davis and the Civil War Era* (Baton Rouge: Louisiana State University Press, 2008), 41–54; Steven E. Woodworth, *Jefferson Davis and His Generals: The Failure of Confederate Command in the West* (Lawrence: University Press of Kansas, 1990) and *No Band of Brothers: Problems in the Rebel High Command* (Columbia: University of Missouri Press, 1999). Koistinen, *Beating Plowshares into Swords*, 102–284, gives a learned and perceptive comparison of Union and Confederate war efforts.

53. On 17 February 1864 the Confederate submarine *H. L. Hunley* sank the screw sloop *Housatonic* off Charleston but was subsequently lost: Tom Chaffin, *The H. L. Hunley: The Secret Hope of the Confederacy* (New York: Hill and Wang, 2008); Brian Hicks and Schuyler Kropf, *Raising the Hunley: The Remarkable History and Recovery of the Lost Confederate Submarine* (New York: Ballantine Books, 2002); Milton F. Perry, *Infernal Machines: The Story of Confederate Submarine and Mine Warfare* (Baton Rouge: Louisiana State University Press, 1965), 90–108; Louis S. Shafer, *Confederate Underwater Warfare: An Illustrated History* (Jefferson NC: McFarland, 1996), 113–25.

54. Hamilton, *Anglo-French Naval Rivalry*, 22–23, 39–46, 88–90, 101, 145, 211; Baxter, *Introduction of the Ironclad Warship*, 23–25, 97–115.

55. See Dull, *French Navy and the Seven Years' War*.

56. R. Arthur Bowler, *Logistics and the Failure of the British Army in America, 1775–1783* (Princeton: Princeton University Press, 1975).

57. A good introduction to Prussia's war against Austria, Russia, Sweden, and France is Franz Szabo, *The Seven Years' War in Europe, 1756–1763* (Harlow: Pearson/Longman, 2008). Frederick II of Prussia, like Lee, was a master of the counteroffensive against rash opponents, but he placed his army in jeopardy when he undertook an offensive into enemy territory. His attacks into Bohemia and Moravia in 1757 and 1758 nearly led to disaster, as did Lee's attacks into Maryland and Pennsylvania in 1862 and 1863. For the rationale behind Confederate offensives, see Joseph L. Harsh, *Confederate Tide Rising* and *Taken at the Flood: Robert E. Lee and Confederate Strategy in the Maryland Campaign of 1862* (Kent OH: Kent State University Press, 1999) as well as the brilliant Robert G. Tanner, *Retreat to Victory? Confederate Strategy Reconsidered* (Washington DC: Scholarly Resources, 2001).

58. The Union blockade greatly increased the wear and tear on Southern railroads, which were forced to substitute for coastal

shipping and river traffic. Moreover, needed rails were removed to armor Confederate ironclads: Surdam, *Northern Naval Supremacy*, 72–84.

59. Thomas Lawrence Connelly, *Autumn of Glory: The Army of Tennessee, 1862–1865* (Baton Rouge: Louisiana State University Press, 1971), 104–105, 306–307, 377–81, 529–32. Ironically, Confederate strategists like General P. G. T. Beauregard were quite familiar with both Prussian military history and the campaigns of Napoleon through the writings of the military theorist Baron Henry Jomini. See Thomas Lawrence Connelly and Archer Jones's penetrating analysis, *The Politics of Command: Factors and Ideas in Confederate Strategy* (Baton Rouge: Louisiana State University Press, 1973) for the failure of the Confederacy to convert theory into practice.

60. For the difficulties of coalition warfare even when successful, see Dominic Lieven, *Russia against Napoleon: The Battle for Europe, 1807–1814* (London: Allen Lane, 2009), 285–528.

EPILOGUE

1. Hoogenboom, *Fox*, 278–86; Niven, *Welles*, 507; Chisholm, *Waiting for Dead Men's Shoes*, 317–35; Schneller, *Quest for Glory*, 329–56; Silverstone, *Civil War Navies*, ix–x; Sprout and Sprout, *Rise of American Naval Power*, 165–66; Koistinen, *Beating Plowshares into Swords*, 173. At war's end the Union navy contained 650 ships, 6,700 officers, and more than 50,000 crewmen. This led to considerable anxiety in Britain and France: Taafe, *Commanding Lincoln's Navy*, xii; Hamilton, *Anglo-French Naval Rivalry*, 307–309. Note that the Quartermaster Department of the Union army also purchased, built, or converted several thousand ships: Koistinen, *Beating Plowshares into Swords*, 146.

2. Chesneau and Kolesnik, *All the World's Fighting Ships*, 125–29. For the deterioration of the navy's ships, see Cornish and Laas, *Lincoln's Lee*, 163–75. For the postwar period, see Chisholm,

Waiting for Dead Men's Shoes, 319–64; Sprout and Sprout, *Rise of American Naval Power*, 166–82; Sloan, *Isherwood*, 159–232; Coletta, *American Secretaries of the Navy*, 1:362–94; Temera Melia Smith, "David Dixon Porter: Fighting Sailor," in James C. Bradford, ed., *Quarterdeck and Bridge: Two Centuries of American Naval Leaders* (Annapolis: Naval Institute Press, 1997), 191–97; and Lance C. Buhl, "Mariners and Mechanics: Resistance to Technological Change in the American Navy, 1865–1869," *Journal of American History* 61 (1974–75): 703–27.

3. Johnson, *Rodgers*, 366–75.

4. Chesneau and Kolesnik, *All the World's Fighting Ships*, 23–24.

5. Chesneau and Kolesnik, *All the World's Fighting Ships*, 137; Paul Kennedy, *The Rise and Fall of the Great Powers: Economic Change and Military Conflict from 1500 to 2000* (New York: Random House, 1987), 200.

6. Chisholm, *Waiting for Dead Men's Shoes*, 365–96; Chesneau and Kolesnik, *All the World's Fighting Ships*, 137–39, 150.

7. For the transition to the new navy, see Peter Karsten, *The Naval Aristocracy: The Golden Age of Annapolis and the Emergence of Modern American Navalism* (New York: Free Press; London: Collier-Macmillan, 1972). The specific causes of the war with Spain are outside the scope of this book, but the general mood of the time was increasingly militaristic and expansionistic: Herring, *From Colony to Superpower*, 299–314.

Index

Studies in War, Society, and the Military

American Naval History, 1607–1865: Overcoming the Colonial Legacy
Jonathan R. Dull

*You Can't Fight Tanks with Bayonets: Psychological Warfare
against the Japanese Army in the Southwest Pacific*
Allison B. Gilmore

*A Strange and Formidable Weapon: British Responses to World War I
Poison Gas*
Marion Girard

Civilians in the Path of War
Edited by Mark Grimsley and Clifford J. Rogers

Picture This: World War I Posters and Visual Culture
Edited and with an introduction by Pearl James

Death Zones and Darling Spies: Seven Years of Vietnam War Reporting
Beverly Deepe Keever

For Home and Country: World War I Propaganda on the Home Front
Celia Malone Kingsbury

I Die with My Country: Perspectives on the Paraguayan War, 1864–1870
Edited by Hendrik Kraay and Thomas L. Whigham

North American Indians in the Great World War
Susan Applegate Krouse
Photographs and original documentation by Joseph K. Dixon

*Citizens More than Soldiers: The Kentucky Militia and
Society in the Early Republic*
Harry S. Laver

*Soldiers as Citizens: Former German Officers in the
Federal Republic of Germany, 1945–1955*
Jay Lockenour

*Deterrence through Strength: British Naval Power and
Foreign Policy under Pax Britannica*
Rebecca Berens Matzke

Army and Empire: British Soldiers on the American Frontier, 1758–1775
Michael N. McConnell

Of Duty Well and Faithfully Done: A History of the
Regular Army in the Civil War
Clayton R. Newell and Charles R. Shrader
With a foreword by Edward M. Coffman

The Militarization of Culture in the Dominican Republic, from the
Captains General to General Trujillo
Valentina Peguero

Arabs at War: Military Effectiveness, 1948–1991
Kenneth M. Pollack

The Politics of Air Power: From Confrontation to Cooperation in Army
Aviation Civil-Military Relations
Rondall R. Rice

Andean Tragedy: Fighting the War of the Pacific, 1879–1884
William F. Sater

The Grand Illusion: The Prussianization of the Chilean Army
William F. Sater and Holger H. Herwig

Sex Crimes under the Wehrmacht
David Raub Snyder

In the School of War
Roger J. Spiller
Foreword by John W. Shy

The Paraguayan War: Volume 1: Causes and Early Conduct
Thomas L. Whigham

The Challenge of Change: Military Institutions
and New Realities, 1918–1941
Edited by Harold R. Winton and David R. Mets

To order or obtain more information on these or other University of Nebraska Press
titles, visit www.nebraskapress.unl.edu.